CW00321623

FESTIVALS AND SAINTS DAYS

A Calendar of Festivals for School and Home

FESTIVALS AND SAINTS·DAYS

A Calendar of Festivals for School and Home

Victor J. Green

BLANDFORD PRESS

POOLE   DORSET

Blandford Press Ltd
Link House, West Street,
Poole, Dorset BH15 1LL

First published 1978
© Blandford Press 1978

Set in Bembo by Dorchester Typesetting
Printed by Biddles of Guildford
Bound by Robert Hartnoll Ltd, Cornwall

ISBN 0 7137 0889 1

ACKNOWLEDGMENTS

Thanks are due to the following for giving generously of time and helpful information:

Mr. Ron Clithero, Head of Religious Education Department at Westminster College, Oxford; Mr. and Mrs. J. Marino; Dr. Kalama Mathur; Miss Julia Mayo; Dr. Charis Waddy; Mr. Arnold Woodley; Miss Vera Frampton; Mr. Terence Goldsmith, Miss Geraldine Christy and Mr. Michael Ridley of Blandford Press; and, in particular, to my wife for so patiently typing and re-typing the manuscript.

Victor Green, B.A., L.G.S.M.

CONTENTS

INTRODUCTION

So that the reverence and the gaiety
May not be forgotten in later experience

T. S. ELIOT

It would be a dull year indeed that had no 'high days and holy days', and these breaks from routine are the more enjoyable if there is some point to them and we become aware of their origins and development. There is a natural curiosity to discover why, when and how the festivals began.

The culture in Britain today is basically Christian and it follows that even in days when attendance at church ceremonial is declining, the calendar of festivals follows the Christian year. However, in view of the increasing number of those with other faiths now making their homes in Britain, some of their festivals are included in this book. There are also one or two festivals with little or no religious significance, as well as American festivals which have associations with Britain. Frequent reference is made to pagan origins of some of the festivals which have been overlaid by later religious observance. This is true not only of Christian festivals but can also be observed in the origins of festivals observed by followers of other faiths. May Day now has its carols and hymns, while the pre-Christian origin of Harvest is lost in the observance of a general thanksgiving for all God's gifts, not only the material produce of the harvest. The Jewish Pesach was probably a spring festival long before it became the Passover, celebrating the flight of the Jews from Egypt.

Festivals develop with time and experience. What started as a rest from labour at spring and autumn attracted ceremonial and ritual that grew out of the observance of nature. As man grew in intellect and reached a higher cultural level, he achieved a greater awareness of the Divine power of God, so that holidays became holy days and ceremonies achieved a new, higher symbolic significance. One would hope that holy days do not revert once more to mere holidays, for that would surely indicate a fall in man's stature.

The interweaving of heathen and Christian elements has developed through Celtic, Roman, Saxon and post-Conquest history. The Pope encouraged Augustine to continue the use of heathen temples, replacing the idol with the Cross, so that the people of England would worship on accustomed sites. He realised the impossibility and impracticability of eliminating all former custom in a moment of time. He did not object to people slaughtering an ox for the feast at a Christian celebration just as they had been used to doing at their former pagan ritual. Indeed the custom of roasting an ox still goes on today. We call it a barbecue. The word 'barbecue' describes the framework or table on which the ox is roasted – possibly an altar?

These customs were not always welcomed by some

clerics and certainly received a set-back in Puritan times. The motivation behind this discouragement of holidays was not solely religious – it sometimes reflected dissatisfaction with industrial and agricultural output. In the 12th century, peasants' holidays amounted to eight weeks of the year, with major festivals occupying the octave, eight days. Christmas headed the list with fun and games continuing until Twelfth Night. While Church attendance was duly observed, it would appear that not all the festivities were reverent.

The 17th century saw the publication of a *Book of Sports* indicating which festivities were sanctioned by the Church, and the Parliament of 1644 went so far as to prohibit the keeping of Christmas. Maypoles were banned, theatres closed and cathedrals threatened with destruction.

Merry England returned with the Restoration to the throne of Charles II, but many festivals were lost and with industrialisation they never returned. Now, with an increase in automation and computerisation, we are experiencing a return to a shorter working week and longer, more frequent holidays. This being so, for Christian and non-believer alike, it is timely to restore traditional Christian festivals which have their roots in the past and emphasize some aspect of Christian practice.

Festivals should not be spectator events – they are events of involvement with significant customs and activities. There is nothing so sad as a child on holiday saying, 'I have nothing to do'.

As well as looking at past customs and activities, this book is also concerned with today's celebrations. Some festivals have been brought to our attention by followers of other faiths now in Britain. What better way of arriving at mutual friendship and understanding than by

3

sharing in their festivals, both grave and joyful? All religions celebrate with a festival of light, their longing for a world that is pure, peaceful and good. We are all seekers of the light, and we know that it comes from one Source. This unites us in a common goal.

The Muslim festivals have been included in the Calendar of Festivals in accordance with the months in which they fall in the calendar year 1978, but it will be appreciated that since the Islamic calendar is based on the orbiting of the moon around the earth, the total number of days in the lunar year is 353, 354 or 355, while the solar calendar has 365 or 366, and any particular date in the Islamic calendar travels backward through the solar calendar, completing a full cycle in about 33 years or about 10 days per year.

NEW YEAR'S DAY   *January 1st*

> *For auld lang syne, my dear,*
> *For auld lang syne,*
> *We'll tak a cup o'kindness yet*
> *For auld lang syne.*
>
> R. BURNS

'A Happy New Year' is a greeting that is worldwide and has been used for as long as time has been recorded, although the actual day on which the new year began has varied from age to age and country to country. Certainly the Romans used the greeting and it was customary for wealthier citizens of Rome to exchange gifts of baskets of dates and figs, garnished with gold leaf. These New Year customs were brought to Britain and, in their turn, the Anglo-Saxons made a feature of welcoming the New Year. So it can be said that the festival has been celebrated in Britain for the greater part of its history.

Everyone likes fresh starts and new opportunities, the chance to resolve to do better and the hope of brighter things in store. New Year and Christmas have competed for popularity since the calendar has been in its present form and the two festivals have never been equally celebrated. In England, Christmas has been the major festival, although as one travels north the emphasis on New Year celebrations increases, until in the border country and in Scotland, certainly since the Reformation, New Year is kept with greater vigour and excitement.

The Church celebrates on January 1st the circumcision of Jesus, his formal acceptance into the Jewish community when he was a young babe. The eight sides of the font

5

at which a child is baptised into the Christian Church remind us of the eight days between the birth of Jesus and the circumcision. John Wesley, bearing in mind those whose thoughts are fixed on the solemnity of the occasion, inaugurated the Watch Night Service and wrote for it a special hymn, *Come let us anew our journey pursue*.

For most, the occasion is one of festivity and crowds of people get together in public places like Trafalgar Square, St Paul's Cathedral steps, and in hotels and ballrooms, where the New Year is welcomed to the strains of *Auld Lang Syne*, often sung badly and incorrectly, except by Scots people. Burns' last line was not 'For the sake of auld lang syne'!

In the court of Elizabeth I the courtiers gave handsomely to the Sovereign, and Ben Jonson in his *Masque of Christmas* introduced a character called 'New Year's Gift' with an orange, a sprig of rosemary and a collar of gingerbread, with gilt on it.

In Scotland, where most of the customs, now to a growing extent duplicated in England, began, the Eve of New Year is called Hogmanay, and the most likely origin of this word is in the Old French 'Au gui l'an neuf' – 'To the mistletoe, the New Year', this being, according to Cotgrove (1611), the Druidical greeting as revellers came from the woods with boughs of mistletoe – the Golden Bough which Aeneas plucked from the oak at the gate of the underworld and which served as a token for safe conduct from one world to the other. The first month of the year was named by the Romans after their god, Janus. This god had two faces, one looking back into the past and another looking forward to the future.

At midnight, at the height of the revelry, comes a

note of solemnity and slight apprehension with the New Year ceremony of 'first footing'. The household, in silence, listens for the stroke of midnight. As the last stroke of the twelve is sounded a loud knock at the door is heard. The door opens, revealing a strange man with dark hair. He enters without greeting and he is seen to be carrying a branch and a sprig of mistletoe. The branch he puts on the fire, the mistletoe on the mantelpiece. Then the silence is broken and he is given wine and cake by the master of the house and all greet each other with the toast, 'Happy New Year'. The stranger may also bring bread, salt and coal, the symbols of hospitality and warmth. He can be offered a piece of silver and usually the stranger takes the mistletoe under which he kisses all the ladies.

Customs vary from place to place, but the symbolism common to them all is not difficult to determine. The stranger represents the new-born year and he comes uninvited and cannot be turned away. Since the festival may well owe its origins to the time when men worshipped the sun as the fount of all new life, the stranger represents the promise of the light and warmth of the sun, made welcome in the darkest days of midwinter.

In many parts of the country the New Year is tolled in on the church bell, or, if there is a peal of bells, the bell-ringers make an effort to mark the occasion with a peal. On one occasion a young lad, whose father had the job of tolling the bell as the New Year came in, went up to the belfry with his father and pleaded to be allowed to toll the first strokes of the New Year. The father agreed and at midnight the boy pulled the bell rope, but so vigorously that the bell itself got hung up and, apart from one half-hearted note, would ring no more. The lad was soundly ticked off, while the villagers remained uncertain for some time as to whether the New Year had begun or not.

Young men used to wait at a sweetheart's door to be the first to greet her in the New Year. Strange night walkers could be invited in to 'first foot', and a strange, dark man might be asked to 'first foot' several times. If no stranger was available, then a member of the household could perform the ceremony, masked.

In recent times a new custom has arisen where the whole party go out just before midnight and all re-enter, following the youngest of the group. This is a variant of an old custom whereby the whole company went out after midnight to wish all people around 'Good Luck' and offer triangular mince-pies known as 'God' cakes which honoured the Trinity.

Another 'goodie' popular at this time was a fruit cake rather like Christmas cake which went by the name of 'ne'erdy cake' or 'New Year's day cake'.

In 1841 Queen Victoria ordered the New Year to be welcomed by a midnight flourish of trumpets. The Queen observed, 'This had a fine solemn effect which quite affected dear Albert, who turned pale, and had tears in his eyes, and pressed my hand very warmly'.

Many would like to celebrate in this way, but trumpeters are rather expensive nowadays.

> 'And there's a hand, my trusty fiere
> And gies a hand o'thine
> And we'll tak a right guid-willie waught,
> For auld lang syne.'

EPIPHANY (TWELFTH NIGHT)   *January 6th*

A cold coming we had of it,
Just the worst time of the year
For a journey, and such a long journey.
                              T. S. ELIOT
                          Journey of the Magi

Epiphany, meaning the appearance or manifestation, celebrates for the Christian the showing of Christ to people other than the Jews. This was the presentation to the three 'magi' or wise men who came from diverse parts of the world to worship Jesus and to present to him significant gifts. This event is re-enacted each year on this day in the Chapel Royal at St James's Palace, London, when the traditional gifts of Gold, Frankincense and Myrrh are ceremonially presented at the altar.

There is a story that when the three wise men first met on their journey to Palestine, the first was convinced that the child was to be a great King and that it was fitting to take a gift of gold. The second was equally sure that the child they were going to greet was to be a great High Priest, to be worshipped over all the world and for him the symbol of praise, incense, would be appropriate. The third wise man said that they were both wrong and that the child would grow up to be the one who would, by sacrifice of his own life, save the world. For such a person, myrrh was correct.

They journeyed together. As they neared the home of the infant Jesus they heard Mary singing the song especially ascribed to her, *The Magnificat*. They listened to the words, 'My soul doth magnify the Lord'. 'Ah,' said the first wise man, 'I was right. He will be a great Lord, a King.' They paused as Mary continued her song,

'My spirit doth rejoice in God'. 'There you are,' said the second, 'He is to be a great High Priest, a God.' Then Mary added, 'My Saviour', and the third wise man congratulated himself on his prophecy that Jesus would be both sacrifice and saviour. They were all correct in their prophesies and all three gifts were significant and appropriate.

Twelfth Day (or Twelfth Night), on which Epiphany falls, is not now marked with the ceremonies accorded to it until just over a century ago. Nowadays the Church has its religious services and where a crib is displayed the figures of the three wise men and their pages or servants are added to complete the Christmas scene.

In most homes the Christmas decorations are taken down on Twelfth Night, the tree, if it has died, is burnt up into grey ash and, if still living, planted carefully in the hope that it will live through the year to be used again next Christmas.

In earlier days Twelfth Night was important enough to be the occasion of a new play by William Shakespeare and parties were held in almost every household. During the day children played in the streets and it was an opportunity for playing tricks on unwary passers-by, rather like All Fools Day. As evening closed in, the pastrycooks' windows gleamed and good trade was had in the sale of 'Twelfth Cakes', large and small, decorated with stars, castles, kings, dragons, palaces and churches in white icing with varied colours.

At each party a king and queen had to be discovered. This was a kind of lottery, for in each cake was hid a bean and a pea. Who found the bean was king, who found the pea was queen. Should the bean be first found by a girl, or the pea first found by a boy, that finder had to choose a partner. Sometimes the pea and bean were replaced by silver coins, say a sixpence and a shilling. At some parties a complete court was elected and due honours paid to the officials.

In country areas up to nearly a hundred years ago, particularly in the cider areas, men and women went out after dark, the men armed with shot guns and one of them carrying a bucket of cider which was set down among the trees. Each man in turn took a cup of cider and after drinking some, poured the remainder over the roots of a tree. He then placed a piece of Twelfth Cake in the fork of the tree 'for the robin'. The company then called out, 'Wes hal' (a modern version is wassail) which meant 'good health'. The men then raised their guns and fired shots in the air. This ceremony was intended to secure a good crop of apples during the coming year.

For all that, Epiphany belongs to the three travellers, wise men, or kings, who made 'such a long journey at the worst time of the year'.

Another story which is not so well known would have us believe that four travellers or kings set out, although only three followed the star.

This other king was called Artaban and he, like the other three, had read the prophecies and studied the heavens and he too set out to find the Saviour. He took with him three precious gifts, an emerald, a ruby, and a pearl, all to be given to this Son of David. As it happened, his way towards Bethlehem lay across a river and as he embarked on a boat to be taken to the far side, he saw a man lying by the wayside. The poor man was evidently very ill and Artaban turned from the boat, which left without him, and went across to the man in need of help. Artaban realised that he needed food and shelter, so he hired a mule to carry the man and went out of his way to get him to an inn where the landlord would look after him. To pay for this care, Artaban gave the innkeeper the emerald intended for the babe. Artaban hurried back to the river, but was now only just able to see the star far ahead. He had lost many valuable days on his journey.

As he approached Bethlehem he had to crouch down in the ditch by the wayside, for a troop of soldiers came galloping along with swords drawn. He followed and was startled by the cries of children and their parents, moaning and shrieking in pain and agony. The soldiers were everywhere, breaking down doors and bringing from the houses the very young, one- and two-year-olds.

Artaban sheltered in a doorway and could hear the sound of crying from inside the house. He pushed his way past the door and saw the frightened mother screening something with her body. She had hidden her child from the soldiers and was afraid for their return. Artaban comforted her and when later a soldier looked in, not wishing to tackle a man, he quickly withdrew, and soon the sound of the retreating troops could be heard. The mother had saved her boy but was dismayed at the damage done to her home. Artaban comforted her and gave her the ruby which was to have been a gift for the child Jesus. With this she would have money to build a new home and a new life for her son.

Artaban heard a rumour that Mary and Joseph and the Baby had escaped to Egypt, so he too travelled there but could not find them.

Artaban heard little about Jesus for nearly thirty years, but always hoped that he would one day see him and present him with the pearl. He heard many stories of his actions and sayings, but somehow never caught up with Jesus.

It was in Jerusalem that he heard that Jesus had been

tried and condemned to death. Could he get to see him just once – could he perhaps help even, with the aid of the precious pearl. On a Friday, he pushed his way through the crowds towards the place where Jesus was to pass on his way to Calvary. Artaban passed through a crowded square where to his horror he found young children being sold as slaves. A heartbroken woman was at his side as one boy was offered. The bidding went on as the mother became more distraught. Just as the sale was going to be made, Artaban stepped forward and bought the boy to restore to his mother. He paid with the pearl. Now he had no gift for Jesus.

Artaban reached the Way of the Cross just as Jesus was passing with His cross. There was a great crowd around and at the windows many people leaned out across the narrow street. From a balcony above Artaban saw a tile dislodged. It hurtled down straight for the head of a young boy. Artaban darted forward in the path of the falling tile, pushing the boy aside. The tile struck Artaban on the head and he fell, knowing that he was dying. Jesus passed at that moment and, with a look that told Artaban that his story of sacrifice was known, said, 'As you have done to others, so you have done it to me'.

Goodmorrow Valentine
I'll be yours
If you'll be mine
Valentine – Valentine

It is difficult to determine who Valentine was, but tradition holds two stories of men put to death for their faith some time during the 3rd century in the reign of the Roman Emperor Claudius II. One was a priest and the other the Bishop of Terni. In all probability this was one and the same man. Valentine evidently resisted un-Christian edicts of the Emperor and for that he was beaten with clubs and beheaded. Claudius had issued an edict that soldiers should not marry, since domesticity reduced their fighting potential, but Valentine performed the marriage ceremony in secret. When he was finally arrested he was thrown into jail and the story goes that he fell in love with the jailer's daughter and she with him. On the day that he was to be led out to his death he left a little note in his cell addressed to her. It was signed, 'Your Valentine'.

Perhaps the allocation of February 14th to this apostle of true love is no accident on the part of the Church, which was alarmed at the perpetuation of activities and rites connected with the pre-Christian Roman festival of Lupercalia on February 15th. These customs were riotous, boisterous and youthful, connected with fertility and new life. It was the day for young men to select the girl of their choice by directly addressing them or by going through some form of lottery whereby the girl did not know which boy was to be hers until the lottery was drawn. Today, 'Valentines' are often left unsigned so that the girl cannot be sure who her Valentine is. Lupercalia was the Roman feast of the wolf and perhaps it is not accidental that we sometimes refer to a young man who pursues the girls as a 'wolf'. Nor is the expression 'wolf whistle' unconnected.

There is another interesting association with a Roman Emperor in that Julius Caesar was offered the kingly crown on the Lupercalia. He suffered from epilepsy, 'The falling sickness'. In some parts of Europe this condition is called St Valentine's Dance.

However, February 14th, with the first stirrings of spring, when birds traditionally choose their mates, was allotted to St Valentine and ever since has drawn to itself customs and usages associated with new love. It was customary in medieval England for young ladies to tie coloured ribbons round their bedheads and eat special, sometimes peculiar, foods to induce dreams of the one who would marry them. There was a tradition that the first unmarried man that a girl met on the morning of this day would become her sweetheart and marry her. Sometimes all the unmarried girls would, on this day, put into a container the names of all the eligible young men and then draw them out to decide whose young man and future husband each boy would be. This method was usually more popular with the plainer girls than with the pretty ones.

The young children found in St Valentine's Day the opportunity for some informal begging in the same way that singing at Hallowe'en and Christmas brought in pocket money. Nowadays the favourite season for this is Guy Fawkes Day. They went around the village singing and chanting usually finishing up with:

> Knock the kettle against the van
> Give us a penny if you can
> We be ragged and you be fine
> Please to give us a Valentine.
> Up with the kettle and down the spout
> Give us a penny and we'll get out.

Children also had a number of games and counting games involving a sort of lottery for kisses; the latest in this fashion was popular many years ago and was known as 'Postman's Knock'.

Oliver Cromwell abolished St Valentine's Day, along with Hogmanay and Hallowe'en, as being altogether too frivolous and irreligious but it soon re-established itself with the Restoration and as well as messages the Valentine also sent gifts. The little cards and letters were usually prettily written with pertinent messages and decorations. The popularity of St Valentine's Day in the 17th century can be judged by the many entries in Samuel Pepys's Diary:

> February 14th, 1661. Up early and to Sir W. Batten's, but could not go in till I asked whether they that opened the door was a man or a woman. But the manservant in a feigned voice answered, 'A woman', which with his tone made me laugh. So up I went and took Mrs. Martha for my Valentine, and then Sir W. Batten he go in the same manner to my wife, and so we were very merry.
> February 14th, 1662. This morning comes in W. Bowyer who was my wife's Valentine, she having held her hands over her eyes all the morning that she might not see the painters who were gilding the chimney piece.

Both these entries refer to the tradition that the first

person you meet that morning of the opposite sex is your Valentine. Although Mrs Pepys took W. Bowyer as her Valentine that year, it is recorded that Sir W. Batten from the previous year sent her 'half a dozen pairs of gloves and a pair of silk stockings and garters'. Gloves, stockings, ribbons and garters were very popular Valentine gifts and were always accompanied by sweet words on a pretty card. An appropriate sentiment with a gift of gloves was:

> Go, little gloves, salute my Valentine
> Which was, which is, which must and
>   shall be mine.
> Love to thee I send these gloves
> If you love me, leave out the 'g'
> And make a pair of loves.

The Valentine letters and, later, cards became more elaborate and popular. Pepys in 1667 wrote about a certain Will Mercer who sent his wife a Valentine with her name 'written on blue paper in gold letters'. These early Valentines were all hand-made.

The 19th century with its printing craftsmen brought the Valentine into common use and with the expansion of the Post Office the Valentine had arrived. In 1825 the Post Office handled two hundred thousand more letters on St Valentine's Day than any other. The Christmas card had not yet become popular. The Penny Post of 1840 and the Half Penny Post of 1870 compelled the Post Office to employ three or four hundred additional workers on February 13th.

With the increased popularity of the Christmas card, Valentines lost their impact and it is only during the past twenty years or so, encouraged to some extent by the makers of greetings cards, that Valentine has come back in favour.

It would be pleasant to think that it is not only the pressure of commercialism that is responsible for the revival of this custom, but a revival of a romantic element essential in human life that was exemplified in that little note left by the saint himself as he went out to his martyrdom, with his simple message, 'Your Valentine'.

MEELAD AL NABI
(Muslim Festival)

12th day of Rabi al Awaal

The believers are brothers
The Koran

This festival is the Muslim celebration of the birthday of the Holy Prophet, Muhammad, and for Muslims it marks the most important event in the history of the world. Muhammad was the 'seal of the prophets', the bearer of the *Koran* and God's final message to mankind. Through him God perfected His religion, Islam. It is a day of festival, of rejoicing, but not of frivolity or pleasure-seeking. Muslim people meet together in assemblies and tell the story of the Prophet's birth, childhood, manhood, character, preachings and sufferings. They also recall his forgiveness of bitter enemies and his final triumph over the hearts of men. Muhammad claimed only to be the last of God's prophets, so that the Muslim attitude to Muhammad is not to be compared with the Christian belief in Jesus Christ, who is revered by them as the Son of God.

The *Koran* tells of many of the patriarchs and prophets of the Old Testament, and the story of Mary and the birth of Jesus is told very simply and reverently in this Muslim Holy Book. The Muslim has five pillars of faith – a witness to God; prayer; giving of alms for the relief of the poor; a discipline of fasting and, if possible, a pilgrimage to Mecca.

The Arabs are descendants of Ishmael, son of Abraham, but they broke up into many tribes and sects, each with their gods and idols of their own. Their beliefs were superstitious and idolatrous, including worship of stone and wood, stars and spirits. The centre of their worship

19

was a rectangular stone building in Mecca about 25 feet (7.62m) high covered with black material and containing effigies and idols for Arabic worship. Arabs made pilgrimages to this place which grew wealthy from the trade brought by pilgrims. One wall of the Ka'ba or Cube, as the building was called, contained a black stone which was the centre of veneration, said to have been sent from heaven to Abraham, and to bear his footprint. The strongest of the tribes and guardians of the Ka'ba and its contents were the Quarish. About A.D. 570, on the twelfth of the Muslim month of Rabi al Awaal, a child was born to the wife of a man called Abdullah of the Quarish tribe. This child was called Muhammad. His father died before he was born and his mother died when he was six. Muhammad lived with his uncle, Abu Talib, and often journeyed with his uncle who was a trader. On one occasion they lodged with a Christian monk called Bahira who declared that the boy would become 'the greatest prophet'.

Muhammad grew up respected for his honesty and wisdom. One story told about Muhammad as a young man concerns the occasion on which the great Ka'ba had to be repaired. When the time came to replace the black stone the various tribes quarrelled as to who should have the honour of doing this. After the wrangling and fighting had lasted several days the Arabs agreed to let the dispute be settled by the first man to visit the holy place on the following morning. Muhammad was the first visitor and the Arabs asked him who should replace the black stone. Muhammad spread out his cloak and the stone was placed on it. He then told the chieftains of each tribe to hold a part of his cloak. Then, as they lifted together, the black stone was restored to its proper place.

Muhammad became the manager of a trading caravan which belonged to Khadija, the widow of a wealthy merchant. He was very successful in this job and eventually when he was twenty-five he married Khadija.

Muhammad was a thoughtful, religious man, and often went off on his own to meditate. The cave of Hira'a on the Mount of Light was a favourite place and one day, as he sat there quietly, he had a vision of an angel carrying a cloth on which was written, 'Read'. 'I cannot read,' said Muhammad. However, the angel insisted and Muhammad read the words after the angel. He returned home very frightened, but his wife urged him to talk with his uncle, Woraka, who was a Christian. Woraka was sure that he had been visited by Gabriel and that these inspired words should be written down. He was also sure that Muhammad had been called to be a prophet of God.

Muhammad received a series of messages which he wrote in a book called the *Koran*. Muhammad began to preach the message of the *Koran* which differed from the religion of the Arabs in that it taught that Allah was One God and that it was wrong to worship many gods. But the men of Mecca who worshipped idols and gained profit from the many pilgrims who came to Mecca plotted to kill Muhammad, who was forced to escape to a city called Medina where some Arabs had already decided to follow the teachings of Muhammad. This journey is called the Hejira and marks the birth of Islam as a religion.

Muhammad was compelled to fight for his faith and led a series of raids against the pagans at Mecca and in A.D. 630 came his final victory. He made Mecca the Holy City of the Muslims, destroyed the idols in the Ka'ba and made it suitable for pilgrims who were to visit Mecca through the ages to come. Two years later Muhammad died.

All the messages received from God by Muhammad were written in the book called the *Koran* although they were not collected together until twenty years after his death. Muslims have a great reverence for their holy book. It must not be put on the ground and many Muslims learn it by heart. It contains stories of Noah, Abraham, Moses, Saul, David and Goliath, Mary and Jesus. Muhammad is seen as the last, but not the only, prophet of God.

The *Koran* instructs Muslims to say:

> We believe in Allah (God) and that which is revealed unto us and that which is revealed unto Abraham and Ishmael and Isaac and Jacob and the tribes, and that which Moses and Jesus received and that which the Prophets received from their Lord. We make no distinction between any of them and unto Him we have surrendered. (Surah 2, v. 136)

The whole life of a Muslim is dedicated to the worship of God.

Saint David is the national saint of Wales and the day set apart in the calendar as St David's day is March 1st, although why this date has been chosen is uncertain. Possibly it commemorates his death which may have been on 1st March A.D. 589. On that day, according to legend, a host of angels bore his spirit to heaven amid great singing to his glory and honour.

David was probably the son of Sandde, a famous prince, and Non, his mother, who ranked as a Cymric saint, in the year 500. He grew up in the Christian faith and was destined to be an important churchman. He took a prominent part in great conferences and assemblies and became the Primate of Wales, a position similar to Archbishop in England. When he was about thirty years old he established a monastery at Glyn Rhosyn which was recognised as the centre of Church government. This place is now called St Davids (Ty Dewi) where the small cathedral city of that name stands. He founded many churches in Wales of which 53 bear his name, although his influence seems to have been much greater in the south than in the north. By the time of the Norman Conquest (1066) his fame had increased and St Davids had become what it still is to this day, a centre of Pilgrimage.

Inevitably, many legends have grown up around the name of the saint. It is said that when David and his monks first came to Glyn Rhosyn the area was terrorised by a brigand named Boca. Even he was overcome by David's personality and became converted to Christianity, although the brigand's wife continued to work against David's influence for a much longer time.

Another story tells us that there was little fresh water

near the monastery but when St David prayed for water, a well sprang up at his feet. Many other wells are said to have sprung up at his wish, often at places like Flynnon Feddyg where he miraculously healed the blind, the lame and the sick.

It is also told that when David was a young man he attended an assembly of bishops at Llanddewibrefi in Cardiganshire where the speakers could not make themselves heard above the noise of the people. David was not to be put off and when he began to speak a hill rose up under him so that from this vantage point all could see and hear him.

Welsh people are proud of their country and many regret the loss of independence and the imposed rule, as they see it, of a foreign country. For this reason the traditional Welsh culture and language is strong, perhaps more emphatic in some parts of Wales than others. This is reflected in the institution of the Royal National Eisteddfod, when musicians, poets, artists and craftsmen gather every year during the first week of August on a site announced a day and a year before. The Archdruid of the Gorsedd of Bards presides and the mythology of the druidic ancestry symbolises that Wales is always 'The Land of my fathers'.

It was in A.D. 700 that the first and only Welsh Prince of Wales, Llywellen the Last, was killed and since then no Welsh Prince, not even Owen Glendower, has been able to restore independence to the Welsh. It now seems possible that an Act of Parliament can do what no battles were able to.

The feeling between the Welsh and English has found expression at times in rhyme and nursery rhyme. Joseph Holliwell in *The Nursery Rhymes of England* 1842 includes verses from 'Taffy was a Welshman', most uncomplimentary to the Welsh, which he says was sung on 1st March in the border areas by English children. Certainly, baiting the Welsh was customary in London on St David's Day.

An early 18th-century chap book, *Taffy's progress to London*, tells how Welsh people were mocked by hanging a bundle of rags from a window representing a Welshman mounted on a red herring with a leek in his mouth.

In Tom Thumb's *Pretty Song Book* (1744) appears this rhyme:

> Taffy was born
> On a Moon Shiny Night
> His head in the Pipkin
> His heels upright.

The poem was accompanied by a picture of a child with his head in a cooking pot.

Tales of theft by the Welsh must have originated during the border wars when probably English farmers found themselves short of a sheep or two after a night raid. No doubt as many Welsh sheep got themselves transferred across the border into England in a similar fashion, although no nursery rhyme commemorates the event.

Today, happily, the feeling is contained by Wales defeating England (or vice-versa) at Twickenham or at Cardiff Arms Park.

Wales has two national emblems – the leek and the daffodil. The leek is a herb of the onion family, but it was worn as a battle emblem by the Welsh against the Saxons, and again by Welsh soldiers at Poitiers. In legend, the leek was said to have the property of carrying its wearer, unscathed, through battle, and was officially worn on the uniform of the Welsh Guards Regiment on St David's Day. Evidently leeks planted when the moon is waning will be small and those planted when the moon is waxing will be large. The Roman Emperor Nero is said to have eaten leeks to clear his voice and the juice of leek is good for sore eyes, rough hands and chilblains, according to folklore.

In recent years the leek has given way to David's flower – Daffodil – and this is appropriate for the daffodil is showing itself at about this time of the year. The name is a corruption of Asphodel which according to Pliny grew on the banks of the Acheron, delighting the spirits of the dead. The Asphodel also grew, according to legend, on the Elysian fields. This may account for the popularity of daffodils on graves. A delightful rhyme is often said:

> Daffadowndilly has come to town
> In a yellow petticoat and a green gown.

By a strange coincidence, in the Isle of Man daffodils are called goose leeks.

In Wales they say that if you are first to find a daffodil in bloom you will have more gold than silver for a year.

HOLI (*Hindu Festival*)   *Early March*

The Hindu religion is one of renunciation, love, peace and kindness, based very largely on family life. Young children get their teaching and training in religion mostly at home, at times supplemented by religious institutions. Each household has its own shrine at which the family worship together.

There is no insistence that Hindus attend communal services at the temple regularly. Those who go to the temple take off their shoes before entering, as a mark of respect. The temples are looked after by the Brahmins, the priestly caste. Originally the Hindus were divided into four main sections or castes on the basis of their functions in society. Brahmins were expected to acquire and impart religious knowledge; Kshatriyas were the guardians of society, trained to rule and fight battles to protect the community; Vaishyas were the traders and the Sudras were to provide the services. These castes are not kept so rigidly today. Some Hindu sects eat only vegetarian food. Hinduism is the main religion of India, and takes several forms. The basic belief is in One Supreme God, Brahma.

The Supreme God is often depicted by three aspects of the One God: Brahma, the creator of the universe; Vishnu looking after the universe, the preserver; Siva, having power to bring the entire creation to an end, when so needed, to redeem the earth from the sins of humanity.

The dependence on natural elements for their existence in the early days led Hindus to create other gods, providing air, water, fire and so on. All are regarded as aspects of the One God. As God is everywhere, in everything, they find this hard to understand and so many gods are created by them to fulfil various functions. There are for example Saraswati, goddess of learning, who is celebrated in schools, and Lakshmi, goddess of wealth and beauty. Hindu temples contain images of one or more of these gods and often families or villages are ardent devotees of a certain god or gods, while maintaining their faith in the supreme Almighty God, Brahma.

Hindus enjoy a calendar of festivals just as Christians do. One of the most important and joyful is Holi which falls on the full moon of the Hindu calendar month Phalguna, usually coinciding with the month of March. This is a fire festival celebrated when the most important crops of the spring harvest are almost ripe, remembering the fertility of the soil and the reinvigoration of the year in springtime. The festival varies in length from place to place but is at least three days in duration. Celebrations often include a procession in which a man dressed as a bridegroom is carried by a donkey through the streets accompanied by a singing, dancing crowd. Humorous titles are often given to more prominent characters in the carnival. The festival begins with lighting a small fire in certain households and a bigger fire for the community which is lit by a Brahman priest. An image of Holika, a legendary character, is made ready to be burnt on the great fire. It used to be customary in the villages for mischievous boys to take anything lying around that would burn and once taken to the fire could not be recovered by the owner. For this reason people cleared everything away from the front or outside of their huts or houses for fear of losing furniture or other goods in the fire. Part of the ceremony included walking round the fire, chanting songs and uttering shouts heralding the festival. Some of the winter barley crop ready at this time is offered to the fire and the roasted barley is eaten at the festival. The ashes of the fire are considered holy and are used as charms.

The second part of the festival includes 'throwing colour'. Coloured dust and coloured water are thrown about and it means good fortune to be sprinkled in this way. Nowadays in the towns, children go round throwing coloured balloons over those taking part in the ceremony, and even in the streets on passers-by.

Holi is a great social festival, a season of goodwill and an occasion for visiting friends, exchanging gifts of sweetmeats and savouries, and making up for past wrongs. People go out of their way to pay or forgive debts and to reconcile quarrels. The bonfires of Holi symbolise the triumph of good over evil, and the burning of rubbish and other articles indicates that past wrong-doing is forgiven and forgotten.

The origins of the festival are explained by numerous legends, too many to be included here. One traces the origin of the fire festival to the day when Siva's anger reduced the god Kama to ashes. Another legend explaining the rituals tells of a king called Hirnakashyah. He was a hard, cruel and unbelieving king who had a son called Prahlad. Prahlad was a great devotee and the boy's adherence to his belief angered the king who tried all ways to make the boy give up his religion. Frustrated by the boy's devotion, he tied Prahlad to a pillar and ordered him to be beaten by his servants. Suddenly the king saw an apparition of the god Narhari, half man and half lion, which frightened the king and the boy was released. Even so, the king was determined to destroy the boy. The king had a sister named Holika who had been made immune from fire by the gods. The king ordered her to take Prahlad in her arms and then both were to be cast into the fire. In that way Prahlad would die and Holika would be saved. What the king did not know was that the gods' charm over Holika was ineffective at a certain hour during the twenty-four-hour day. The time chosen for lighting the fire happened to be at this very time and so when the flames leapt up Holika died but Prahlad was saved.

So Holi is a festival of joy when the power of Prahlad's devotion overcame the evil of Holika and Hirnakashyah.

Saint Patrick is the patron saint of Ireland. As one might expect with a saint who lived in the 4th century, there are conflicting accounts of his life and a great number of legends about him. Two important documents are said to have been written by Patrick and from these we can find something of the story and personality of the man. One of these is *The Confession*, giving an account of his life, and the other is *The Letter to Coroticus*, which tells us something of his style, personality and methods when urging Christian subjects to stand up against pagan leaders.

Patrick was born about A.D. 389, the son of a middle-class landowner who brought his son up as a Christian, a course not without its dangers in a largely pagan community. St Alban was martyred for his Christian belief in A.D. 287. Patrick is said to have lived at a place called Bannaventa which might correspond with Daventry, but it is more likely to have been at Banwen in Glamorganshire.

When he was sixteen a band of marauding Irish captured him and took him back to Ireland as a slave. He was made to look after sheep owned by a chieftain called Milince in County Antrim. During the six years of his captivity his Christian belief sustained him and he resolved to give his life to the cause of his religion. He made his escape to Wicklow and boarded a ship engaged in the trade of exporting Irish wolf-dogs. He was put off on the coast of Gaul and made his way to the monastery at Lerins where he spent a few years. After that he returned to his home in Britain and conceived the idea of a Christian mission to Ireland. He described how in a dream he saw a man named 'Victorious' holding

31

letters from Ireland and gave him one which he read. The words in the letter began 'The Voice of the Irish', and the voice said, 'We pray you, holy youth, to come again and walk among us as before'.

Patrick returned to Gaul to the monastery at Auxerre where he was ordained by Bishop Amator, and for fourteen years prepared for his vocation as a missionary to Ireland.

In 432 Patrick returned to Ireland and, although there are conflicting stories about where he started his missionary work, he probably landed at Inverdea in Wicklow and proceeded to East Ulster, the kingdom of Ulidea. Patrick realised that to succeed he needed the goodwill of the tribal kings and the clan chieftains.

He succeeded in converting one chieftain named Dichu who gave him a site on which to establish a place of worship, a wooden barn. This place was called Saul; the Irish name for a barn is 'saball'.

The most powerful chief was the High King of Tara, who ruled supreme over all the others. He had ordered that every fire in Ireland must be put out at Easter and relighted from a fire in the King's own castle, and that those who disobeyed would be put to death. One Easter he looked out and there, on an opposite hill, was a fire blazing away. Patrick had deliberately lit it, as he explained when he was seized and brought before the High King, as a sign that Christ who rose from the dead was the Light of the World. He was set free, which showed both the strength of his conviction and that of the Christian community. Patrick travelled throughout Ireland, founding churches and forming communities, including the church and monastery at Armagh. He died in A.D. 461 and was probably buried at Saul.

Inevitably, around such a figure many traditional legends have grown, the most famous of which is his use of the shamrock to illustrate the mystery of the Trinity, the three-in-one. He was having some difficulty in teaching the Unity of God in the three persons of Father, Son and Holy Spirit, when he bent down and picked a shamrock leaf. This he held out to those watching and listening and showed them that in the one leaf there were three parts, all separate yet all part of the one. From then on the shamrock became the emblem of the Irish and few Irish people would leave their country without taking a piece of shamrock or clover with them. To find a four-leaf clover is considered lucky indeed, but this may be a Christianised version of a Celtic lucky charm of three figures (triquetra) enclosed in a fourth, the ancient Celtic sun wheel.

There is a legend connecting Patrick with Joseph of Arimathea. This tells that Joseph came to England after the death of Jesus bringing with him the Sangreal, or dish used at the Last Supper. This disappeared, never to be found again, although many stories have been told of the search for the Holy Grail. Joseph, while in England, built a little chapel on the spot where later was built Glastonbury Abbey. Patrick is said to have founded a monastic community there. Norton, in Northamptonshire, also claims to be the home of Patrick, but this is difficult to substantiate.

One legend concerning his resolve to convert the Irish people to Christianity asserts that, while in bondage in Ireland, he was resting on a hillside. A huge boulder came hurtling down on to him that must have killed him. Amazingly, the boulder split in two and each of the pieces fell on either side of Patrick. By this he knew that he had been saved to lead a mission to Ireland.

There is a story at Glyn Rhozyn in Pembrokeshire that Patrick came there to settle but, in a dream, an angel told him to move on since this place was being reserved for St David, the patron saint of Wales.

Another legend claims that Patrick ministered in Dumbarton near Glasgow. He was so successful that the Devil ordered every witch to rise up against him. He fled to the Clyde and took ship for Ireland. Since witches cannot cross water, they tore huge boulders from the hills and threw them after him. The biggest of these missed Patrick and fell, to become the rock on which Dumbarton Castle was built.

The Irish flag, a diagonal red cross on a white background, became part of the Union Flag in 1801.

Saint Patrick's Breastplate

I bind unto myself today
   The power of God to hold and lead,
His eye to watch, His might to stay,
   His ear to hearken to my need,
The wisdom of my God to teach,
   His hand to guide, His shield to ward,
The word of God to give me speech,
   His heavenly host to be my guard.

SHROVE TUESDAY
ASH WEDNESDAY
SEASON OF LENT

The Church's year, reflecting the life of its people, must have its high, exciting and uplifting times together with the calmer, reflective and meditative moments. After Christmas comes a time concerned with getting to grips with the rigours of winter and then, as the days lengthen and the sun creeps higher in the sky, before the outburst of spring heralding the joyous festival of Easter, comes a period of self-denial, penitence and quiet reflection. Shrovetide is the messenger of this quiet time. Easter would be meaningless without Good Friday; Good Friday demands quiet, penitential preparation.

Shrove Tuesday cannot be fixed as a date on the calendar because Easter Sunday has its connection with the Jewish Feast of the Passover and the sacrifice of the Paschal Lamb. This in turn is determined by the Paschal full moon which of course varies in the date of its appearance, so that Easter may fall on any date from March 22nd to April 25th. It follows that all the other festivals dependent on the timing of Easter are variable to that extent. These include Shrovetide, Lent, Mothering Sunday, Easter and Whitsun. There has been discussion between the churches with a view to fixing the date of Easter and this may well be done in due course. It is likely to be fixed on, say, the first or second Sunday in April.

Shrovetide is preceded by three Sundays, named Septuagesima, Sexagesima, Quinquagesima, which roughly estimate the number of days to Easter; seventy, sixty, fifty, but since they come at seven-day intervals can hardly be seen to have mathematical accuracy. For less time-orientated folk it was near enough; to our 'time signal' and 'time-table' dominated society the convention appears quaint. The penitential season of Lent lasts forty days, not counting Sundays, its length significantly connected with the forty days spent in the wilderness by Our Lord in his preparation for his ministry. However, the few days before the solemn season may be spent joyfully as well as in solemn preparation. One aspect of this preparation was to confess misdoings to a priest and ask through him for God's forgiveness. The priest would convey absolution and impose a penance. This practice continues in the Christian Church, possibly more universally observed by Roman Catholics than by Anglicans and others. The Anglo-Saxon word 'scrifan' meant 'to shrive' or 'to impose a penance'. The past tense of the verb 'shrove' affords the name for this Tuesday before Lent begins.

Originally Shrovetide included Quadragesima Sunday, Shrove Monday and Shrove Tuesday. Before the solemnity of Lent there was need for an outburst of jollification, of which many forms have survived. The fasting during Lent forbade eating certain foods and any of these remaining in the larder had to be cleared by Shrove Tuesday. On Shrove Monday or Collop Monday as it was sometimes known (a collop is a specially prepared slice of meat) the housewife used up all the meats that were not to be eaten during Lent and on Shrove Tuesday all the fats and cream had to be finished up and traditionally they were put into pancakes. This eating was accompanied by all kinds of games, frolics and festivities, many of which have survived. Happily cock fighting has been outlawed, but street football, tugs-of-war, and other activities have been perpetuated. In France this is 'Mardi-Gras', Fat Tuesday; in Germany it

is 'Fastendienstag'. Shrove Tuesday was regarded as a
holiday for apprentices and in Henry Bournes' *Antiquities*
(1725) they were warned. that they ought 'with that
watchful jealousy of their ancient rights and liberties,
which becomes the young Englishman, to guard against
every infringement of its ceremonies, and transmit
them entire and unadulterated to posterity'. This they
evidently failed to do, and this is one holiday that got
away.

In many towns the festival is celebrated with physical
contests of a particularly violent nature, often played as a
ball game between two sides of unlimited number. The
most notable takes place in Ashbourne in Derbyshire
where Uptown plays Downtown throughout the day.
Anyone can join in and, since the contest is so violent,
house and shop fronts along the High Street have to be
boarded up. It would be easy to see in this some pagan
struggle between the forces of good and evil, as one
could also interpret a tug-of-war, but there is no evidence
to support this theory.

While the ball game was in progress children used to
shout:

> Pancakes and fritters
> Say All Saints and St Peters
> When will the ball come
> Says the bell of St. Alkum
> At two they will throw
> Says Saint Warabo.

At Westminster School there is an annual ceremony
of 'tossing the pancake'. The school cook, carrying a
pancake in a pan, heads a procession into the Great Hall
where a high bar runs from wall to wall separating
upper from lower school. The competitors, one student

from each form, line up under the bar. At a sign from the Headmaster, the cook tosses the pancake over the bar. A wild scrimmage for pieces of pancake ensues and after two minutes the Headmaster calls 'time'. The origin of this 'Pancake Greaze' as it is called is not known but it is certainly more than two centuries old.

The people of Olney in Buckinghamshire celebrate Shrovetide with their famous pancake race. This is open to women over 18 who have lived in Olney for at least three months. Each competitor in bonnet and apron runs from the market square to the church, about a quarter of a mile, with a pan holding a pancake, which must be tossed three times. The winner is kissed by the verger and, with the runner-up, receives a prayer book. All competitors attend a service when Olney hymns are sung. The event dates back about 350 years and is said to have originated when a housewife, cooking pancakes, heard the church bell for service and rushed off still clutching her pan with a pancake in it. The event, which had lapsed, was revived in 1947.

With the fun of Shrove Tuesday completed, the solemn season of Lent begins with Ash Wednesday. The medieval church had very severe rules of fasting and penitence which have changed from time to time but generally have become more relaxed. At one time no meat could be eaten during Lent – the fishmongers prospered and each monastery wisely kept a fish pond. Until quite recently the Church insisted on abstinence from eating meat on Wednesdays and Fridays through-out Lent, but today the rule is observed only on Ash Wednesday and Good Friday. These rules are more commonly observed in the Roman Catholic Church than in the Anglican community. The Church now emphasizes the need for reflection and meditation, a renewal of faith and self-examination in matters of self-ishness, lack of care for others and missed opportunities.

The name Ash Wednesday derives from an ancient ceremony in which a sinner made public penance by appearing before the congregation clad in sackcloth and covered with ashes. The Old Testament prophets wrote of the even earlier penance of 'sackcloth and ashes'.

The present-day service observed in the Catholic Church uses ashes obtained by burning the palm crosses which had been used the previous year in the ceremonies of Palm Sunday. These ashes are placed in a bowl and, after a blessing and sprinkling with holy water, they are used by the priest to mark a cross with his thumb on the foreheads of those present. As he does so he says: 'Remember, man, that thou art dust and unto dust shalt thou return'. A reflection of the words in the burial service – 'Ashes to ashes, dust to dust'.

The word Lent is derived from the same root as our word 'length', and the fast took its name from the season of the year when the days begin to grow longer. Mention has been made of the fasting regulations and it is interesting to note that from time to time abstinence from eating meat was not always imposed with a religious motive. When the fasting rules were beginning to be relaxed the fisherman had something to say. They found support in Parliament in 1562 when Lord Cecil persuaded Parliament to pass a 'politic ordinance on fish eating' which made meat eating on a fast day punishable by a fine of three pounds or three months' imprisonment.

In Puritan times, militant protestants were ostentatious in their avoidance of a fish diet. A contemporary writer stated, 'that if any superfluous feasting, or gormondizing, or paunch-cramming assembly do meet, it is so ordered that it must be either in Lent, upon a Friday, or a fasting, for the meat does not relish well except it be sauced with disobedience and contempt of authority'.

However, the Church realised that a slight let-up was needed in the middle of Lent and, in consequence, Refreshment Sunday or Mothering Sunday was instituted.

MOTHERING SUNDAY –   *Britain – Mid-Lent*
MOTHER'S DAY   *USA – Second Sunday*
REFRESHMENT SUNDAY   *in May*

> *I'll to thee a Simnel bring,*
> *'Gainst thou go a-Mothering,*
> *So that when she blesseth thee*
> *Half the blessing thou'll give me.*

ROBERT HERRICK (1591-1674)

With the solemn season of Lent half gone, the Church, in its calendar, allows a slight let-up in its Lenten fasting and other austerities. The Gospel of the appointed day tells the story of the feeding of the five thousand and so, appropriately, the day became known as Refreshment Sunday. The Church in its early years had a special ordinance requiring priest and people to visit the Mother church of the district on this day and this ecclesiastical custom became associated with pleasant gatherings of families and reunions of children with their mothers. Hence the popular name for this day is 'Mothering Sunday'.

By the 17th and 18th centuries it was common practice for serving maids and apprentices to be given a holiday on this day so that they might visit their mothers. These servants and apprentices probably left their own homes by the time they had reached ten years of age and from then on lived in accommodation provided by the master. Mothering Sunday would be the only day in the year on which they would see their families and retain the very tenuous links with home. They took gifts of flowers or special cakes made for the occasion. These cakes were spicy and made with a fine flour which had a Latin name, 'simila', hence the cakes were known as Simnel cakes. This is the generally accepted derivation of 'Simnel', but in All Saints Church at Leighton Buzzard, Bedfordshire, there is a carving on one of the pillars which dates from the 15th century, which is thought by some to show the mythical figures of Simon and Nell who made the first Simnel cake.

There appear to have been three varieties of this cake each named after a town. Shrewsbury Simnel had a thick crust, Devizes Simnel was baked in the shape of a star without crust, while Bury Simnel was flat, rising in the middle. All were made with fine flour, currants, peel and spice. The fashion of having such cakes on this day is returning, the cakes now being decorated with little fruits, artificial flowers with eggs and nests – a look forward to the great church festival of Easter.

All this has little to do with Mother's Day, although in England the days now coincide. Mother's Day is directly connected with the mother of the family, while Mothering Sunday is focused first on Mother Church and incidentally on the family relationship.

Mother's Day is an American institution. On 9 May 1906, a certain Miss Anna Jarvis of Philadelphia lost her mother. On the first anniversary she invited a friend to visit her and declared that she wanted to induce American people to set aside a day when mothers would be honoured and remembered. She talked to influential people and wrote letters to public people detailing her scheme. She succeeded in persuading the governors of Philadelphia to proclaim the second Sunday in May to be Mother's Day. Her influence spread wider and State after State fell into line. In Pennsylvania – a State holiday; in Texas – a day of pardon for some prisoners; in churches – services; in schools – making gifts and cards for Mother. In 1913 the Senate and the House of Representatives officially dedicated the day 'to the memory of the best mother in the world – *Your* mother'.

In the United States of America Mother's Day is possibly less connected with the Church as a religious festival. A fuss is made of mother who receives presents of candy or flowers and is absolved from some of the chores of housekeeping. She may receive greetings cards from children who cannot be with her on the day and possibly is taken out to dinner. There is also in some parts a custom of wearing a flower in the dress or button-hole, red if mother is still alive, or white to indicate that mother has died but is far from forgotten.

During the Second World War many American servicemen over in Britain were surprised that the British did not mark a special day as Mother's Day. They often adopted their British hostesses as a kind of foster mother and on this day gave presents and flowers to show their appreciation of the hospitality they enjoyed. When the American servicemen went back to their homeland they left behind this pleasant practice, and it was happily made to coincide with Mothering Sunday. Indeed, the two practices have merged and presented to all the opportunity of devoting a special day to the renewal of the joy of home life and the unity of the family, for many within the orbit of Mother Church.

APRIL FOOLS' DAY   *April 1st*

> *The first of April, some do say,*
> *Is set apart for All Fools' Day;*
> *But why the people call it so,*
> *Nor I, nor they themselves do know.*
>
> Poor Robin's Almanack 1760

This name, given to the first day in April, reflects the custom of playing tricks on other people or sending them off on fools' errands. The origins of these practices are difficult to determine but April fooling may have had some connection with the ancient celebrations of the equinox, again terminating about April 1st. Another theory is that the fooling became customary when in 1564 the French decreed that the New Year began on January 1st as opposed to April 1st, so that New Year gifts and cards which had been a feature of April 1st were transferred to January. For a joke, some people continued to send mock gifts and cards on April 1st.

The joking on April 1st in England does not seem to have been customary until the 18th century. In Scotland the fooling is sometimes called 'hunting the gowk', or cuckoo, and April Fools were known as 'April Gowks'.

Fools are not always figures of fun, as is evident when the fools in Shakespeare's plays are considered. The Fool in *King Lear* has some of the wisest lines allotted to him, and Touchstone in *As You Like It* is no fool with his 'great heap of knowledge'. The Fools in the Sword Dances and Morris Dances no longer appear funny to modern sophisticated eyes, but all come to us from characters that were serious originally; the Fool is always a butt or victim.

The 'silly season' is from midnight to midday on

April 1st, formerly the first twelve hours of the New Year. The object is to discomfort the victim and if possible send him on a fool's errand or tempt him into a response which indicates that the fool has believed something which is untrue. How many shoe laces are said to be untied on this particular morning each year? How many invisible smuts appear on faces? How many victims are sent to buy a pot of striped paint, or tenpence worth of strap oil – to be delivered on that part of the anatomy ordained by nature to be strapped?

More ambitious, contrived fools' errands have been recorded, as in 1860 when a great number of people received invitations to a reception at the Tower of London – 'To admit bearer and friend to view the annual ceremony of washing the white lions'. Many people actually attended.

One of the great hoaxes of all time, though not in fact perpetrated on April 1st, was on the occasion when members and friends of the Stephen family (Virginia Woolf was one of those involved) persuaded the Royal Navy to make arrangements for a party of important people from the Middle East (played in costumes and make-up by the Stephens) to be conducted over one of His Majesty's warships and provided with full hospitality.

An April Fool catch which involved millions of viewers was the Richard Dimbleby TV programme about the spaghetti harvest in Italy, with a film of long strips of spaghetti being collected by farm workers from the trees.

At twelve noon, all is over. Any trick played after that hour falls back on the head of the jester. In these circumstances the proposed victim uses the age-old formula:

> April Fools' Day's past and gone,
> You're the Fool and I am none.

PALM SUNDAY
HOLY WEEK

> *There was a shout about my ears*
> *And palms before my feet.*
>
> G. K. CHESTERTON
> *The Donkey*

Palm Sunday is the first day of Holy Week, the Sunday before Easter and the opening of the most dramatic week in the Christian year. It celebrates the entry of Jesus into Jerusalem, knowing that by the end of the week he would be cruelly killed. Jesus made this journey on the back of a donkey, with crowds of people, gathered to celebrate the Jewish Passover, lining the road with palm branches, waving palms in the air and crying 'Hosannah to the Son of David'.

The donkey figures in many incidents in Our Lord's life and the mark of the cross on the donkey's back is said to have originated on the first Palm Sunday. A donkey carried Mary to Bethlehem just before Jesus was born; a donkey took Mary and her babe to safety in Egypt and then brought the family safely back to Nazareth. The donkey appears as a leading character in numerous folk tales. Aesop wrote 27 fables about the donkey and at one time Greek and Roman writers accused Christians of worshipping the donkey.

In times past, when English life was more rural, on this Sunday the country folk went out to cut and bring back into the house long wands of willow together with branches of box. This was called 'a-palming' although no palm grew in this country. The men carried slips of willow and wore buds of willow in their hats and buttonholes. The willow was chosen because it was the most advanced of trees at this time of the year. The church services of the day did, and in some places still do, re-enact the story of Palm Sunday with processions into and round the church. There was a medieval ceremony in which two groups circled the church in opposite directions. One group was led by a cross covered with material, while the second group followed a glittering, jewelled cross. When the groups met the hidden cross was carried away to the sounds of victorious shouts and singing, and the fine cross was carried aloft while branches of willow and flowers were thrown down to make a path. As with many of these events held in the churchyard, this led to a good deal of fooling and merry-making, until the Church discouraged it. Even so, many church ceremonies on this day still include solemn processions with palms, and there is a distribution of strips of palm, looped and folded into the form of a cross. These palms are preserved in church and in homes until the next Ash Wednesday when they are burnt to provide ashes for the ceremonies marking the beginning of Lent.

One impressive feature of the Palm Sunday cere-monies in some church services is the dramatic reading or singing of the story of the last week of Christ's life known as 'The Passion'. Three deacons take the parts to be enacted, one singing the words attributed to Jesus, one sings the narrative, while the third sings the words of the crowd and other characters. The choir can join in with the crowd parts. This was, in some churches, sung from the rood loft, which was an open space above the chancel used as a store room. It could often be reached by a stone stairway built into a buttress and a fine example of this can be seen at St Clement's Church, Leigh-on-Sea, Essex. It is interesting to note that these rood lofts may have been the first permanent stages for dramatic performance. Later the rood loft gave way to a rood beam or rood screen on which were displayed in the form of a dramatic scene, the figures of St John the Divine and Mary, the mother of Jesus, regarding Jesus on the Cross.

Throughout Holy Week, that is from Palm Sunday to Maundy Thursday, the Church in its selected readings re-enacts the incidents of that week. Early in the week Jesus turned out the merchants and money-changers from the Temple. He was protesting against the mis-use of the Temple by merchants making gain from the Jews gathering in Jerusalem for the Passover. To buy creatures for sacrifice, the Jew needed Temple money and the money-changers were demanding unfair fees. The visits to the Temple are followed carefully; the trick question of tribute due to Caesar and God; the value of the widow's mite; the precious ointment poured over the feet of Jesus by Mary Magdalen; the bargaining by Judas over his fee for the betrayal; the preparation for the festival of the Jewish Passover which was to presage the central service of the Christian faith, variously called Communion, Eucharist and Mass.

Mention has been made of incidents in Jesus' life that involved a donkey, and it might be appropriate to retell a lovely story about a donkey that Fr Bernard Walke tells in his book *Twenty Years at St. Hilary*. Normally, donkeys do not form undying friendship with man, as dogs and horses do, but Billy was an exception. Not that Billy was completely predictable. He was owned by the parish priest of a little village in Cornwall and had quite an affectionate nature which he tried to hide under a jaunty, independent manner. He had a habit of gathering a band of like-minded donkeys and leading them

48

through gardens and cabbage patches on a minor rampage. He was good at opening gates and avoiding capture, two valuable assets in any donkey.

However, as he got older he had to give up this sort of activity and became rather lonely, but each year seemed to become his younger self round about Christmas time when it was a ritual on Christmas Eve for the family to put out a special feed of corn under a Christmas Tree set up in the courtyard.

Then came an opportunity to let him go to a vicarage in another village about three miles away, by the sea, where the vicar had several young children. Billy was a little sad at first, but soon enjoyed the romps along the sand with the children taking turns on his back. But he did not forget his old home.

The first Christmas Eve after his move, just as the Vicar, who had been the former owner of Billy, was preparing to go over to the church for the midnight service, his maid rushed into the room calling, 'Please, Billy has come to spend Christmas'. There was Billy, standing by the tree in the courtyard waiting for his special feed of corn.

Billy lived to see three more Christmasses and every Christmas Eve found him waiting by the tree for his feed. What sort of intelligence allowed him to figure out the calendar and reckon up which day was December 24th? Moreover, one of the years was a leap year!

PESACH (PASSOVER)
Jewish Festival

April

> *Let my people go, that they may serve me.*
>
> Exodus 9.i

'Pesach', usually called the Passover, is the greatest of the Jewish festivals, *the* holiday of the year and the oldest in the Jewish calendar. Like the Christian Easter, it varies in date from year to year, but occurs in spring and lasts for seven or eight days, not all of which are taken as holidays.

The festival probably dates back to the time when the Jews were wandering shepherds in the deserts of the Middle East, pitching their tents wherever they found grazing for their flocks. At the time of the year when the young lambs were born, they observed a festival at which either a sheep or goat was sacrificed as a way of giving thanks; they gave up something which was valuable to them. The sacrifice was given at nightfall and the animal roasted whole and eaten hurriedly. No bones of the animal could be broken and no meat should be left uneaten by daybreak. As protection against ill luck the tent posts were daubed with the blood of the creature. It was a family affair, not connected with the priests or the place of worship.

It seems that other groups of Jews who were more settled and lived by tending the earth and growing crops had a festival of their own in springtime, which took place before they harvested the barley. This festival was called the 'Feast of Unleavened Bread', that is bread which had no yeast or leavening. At the beginning of the festival all sour doughs, used like yeast to leaven the bread, had to be destroyed to safeguard the produce of the year to come. Then the first sheaf of the newly-cut barley, the 'omer' was presented, as a sacrifice of thanks-giving, to the priest. These people, of course, did not move from place to place like the shepherds and so had more permanent places of worship, the 'high place' on a hill.

Even so, there were years of poor harvests and the Jews found themselves dependent on the Egyptians for corn during the poorer years. Thanks to a Jew named Joseph who had been sold into slavery in Egypt, but had risen to a position of authority, the Jews moved into Egypt to share good harvests, and increased in numbers and in authority. This did not please the successive Kings or Pharoahs of Egypt and gradually the Jews found themselves reduced to abject slavery and longed to be free to reach 'The land promised to them by God'. Under the leadership of Moses, the Jews achieved their freedom and the occasion of their exodus was a terrible punishment on the Egyptians, when the first born of every family died in a single night. This punishment 'passed over' the houses of the Jews and, led by Moses, the Jews set out to find their 'land flowing with milk and honey'. Ever since that time, Jews have remembered the night when they ate hurriedly, ready for the journey, and painted the doorposts of their houses with the blood of the lamb so that the plague of death did not touch the house.

The two festivals of 'Pesach' and 'Unleavened Bread' have combined in the ceremonial of 'The Passover' and the two spring festivals become one historical festival symbolising the struggle of the Jewish people towards national freedom.

In the early days of Jewish history it was a Pilgrimage festival when all who could made their way to the

Temple in Jerusalem. After the destruction of the Temple and as Jews were more widely dispersed over the world, the festival divided into two parts, the ceremonial in the local Temple, the synagogue, and the observance in each home.

For the festival, the home is made spotlessly clean and, on the eve of the Passover, all leavened bread is destroyed while 'matsoh' or unleavened bread is prepared. Greetings are exchanged, the home is filled with light, and the meal for the eve of the Passover is set while the entire family sits around the table. This meal is called the 'Seder' and the various parts of it remind the Jews of the deliverance from the cruelty and enslavement in Egypt. At the commencement the youngest son asks four traditional questions which his father answers fully. In this way the younger generation is taught.

The meal itself has special items in it. Four cups of wine are taken, possibly connected with the four cups of wine in the dream of the Pharaoh's butler which Joseph interpreted. There are cakes of bread, roasted egg, a dish of salt water, perhaps representing the tears of the Jews in bondage, bitter herbs and a sweet paste of almonds, apple and wine, said to represent the clay with which the Israelites were forced to make bricks when they were slaves.

There are up to fourteen parts to the ceremonial of the Seder. It has given rise to inspired works of art in the making of Seder dishes, Passover banners and matsoh covers. Christians are interested in this meal, for it was probably at the Seder that Jesus took the cup and the bread at one point and instituted what for Christians became the centre point of their religion, 'The Last Supper', now in Christian worship called 'Communion', 'The Eucharist', or 'The Mass'.

The last part of the Seder consists of prayers and songs, and a cup of wine is poured symbolically for Elijah, when the door is left open so that he may enter and drink.

Pesach or Passover has a long history, but for Jews it remains essentially a family festival when the whole family comes together to remember, to rejoice, and especially to hear again the wonderful story of their deliverance, and to look forward to the time when all over the world they enjoy freedom once more. In Jewish tradition the festival is known as 'The Season of Release'. Its central theme is 'release' and this can be interpreted on three levels. Historically the Passover celebrates the exodus of the Israelites from Egypt. On the annual seasonal level it marks the release of the earth from the tight grip of winter, and on a personal level, for each of those taking part, it symbolises his or her hope of release from the bondage of wrongdoing.

MAUNDY THURSDAY
GOOD FRIDAY

Maundy Thursday is so named from the words of Jesus when, at the feast of the Passover, the meal commonly called by Christians the Last Supper, he said that he gave them a new commandment. He spoke the words as he proceeded to his act of humility and service, washing his disciples' feet. The Latin words are, 'Mandatum novum da vobis' – 'A new commandment I give you'. From the first word 'mandatum' has come 'maundy'.

For many years the special service on this day included washing the feet of some parishioners by the priest. Indeed St Oswald, Archbishop of York from A.D. 972–992, insisted on washing the feet of twelve poor men every day. Aelfric, Archbishop of Canterbury from A.D. 996–1006, decided that once a week, on Thursday, was enough for his monks, and that only for one another and not for poor visitors. Sir Thomas More stated that Henry VIII washed the feet of as many poor men as he himself was years old and also gave gifts of food and money. Queen Elizabeth I also washed the feet of paupers, but only after they had first been scrubbed clean in herb-scented water.

The ceremony of washing by the Sovereign was discontinued in 1754, but the practice of coining special Maundy Money to be distributed by the Sovereign at Westminster Abbey goes on to this day and sets of Maundy Money will now fetch high prices as collector's items. The Yeomen of the Guard accompany the Sovereign on this occasion, one of them carrying a dish bearing the purses. The Sovereign and all other members of the procession carry little nosegays of scented flowers, a reminder of the days when such precautions were considered necessary against smells and infection by the Plague. The number of sets is always the same as the age of the Sovereign.

The day has also been known as Shere (Clean) Thursday, referring possibly to the washing ceremonies or to the fact that after the Maundy Thursday ceremonies the altar of the church was left clean and bare. Since there would be no consecration of bread at the Good Friday ceremony, the Maundy Thursday service ends with a procession to a specially prepared altar, ablaze with lights, where some of the wafers or bread are deposited to be watched over through the night. This is to recall the solemnity of that evening when Jesus was betrayed while his disciples slept. 'Could you not watch with me one hour,' he said. Many medieval churches had a special altar of repose, or 'Easter Altar', before which this vigil could be kept.

So to the dawn of Good Friday which commemorates the trial and crucifixion of Jesus. One is tempted to say, 'What was Good about that?' Of course it was a black day, but the Christian knows that without the events of that Friday there could have been no Easter.

For many of us the pleasant memory of Good Friday is that we eat hot cross buns which in former years were brought round by street vendors calling, 'Hot Cross Buns – one a penny; two a penny; Hot Cross Buns'. This seemingly trivial Christian reminder of the fate of Jesus is not completely Christian, but rather another example of grafting Christian tradition on to an older pagan one. Two loaves, each marked with a cross, were found among the ashes of Herculanium which was destroyed in A.D. 75 and it is unlikely that they were made for a Christian. The Greeks also marked cakes in this way, but more significantly the Anglo-Saxons made small cakes marked with a cross at the Spring Festival held in honour of Diana. In Hertfordshire, where Ermine Street crossed Icknield Way in Roman times, the ruins of an altar have been found which was raised in honour of Diana of the Crossroads. By co-incidence the area is noted for making good Hot Cross Buns.

The services of the church remind Christians of the events of the first Good Friday. The sacred bread is brought back from the altar of repose and consumed, the cross is uncovered and many services recall the last words of Our Lord, the seven 'words' from the Cross. Then the undecorated church is left silent, mourning the death of Jesus yet anticipating the joy of Easter.

Good Friday has become a fashionable day on which to perform what are known as Passion Plays, plays re-enacting the events of the last week of the life of Jesus Christ. Perhaps the most famous of these is that performed at Oberammergau (although this is now performed in summer time when more people have the opportunity of seeing it) in memory of a time during the middle ages when the village survived a great plague that swept across Germany. The people of the village resolved to perform this play every ten years. This they have done and the play now has world-wide fame. Some 400 performers take part and auditions and rehearsals begin two years before the date of perform-ance. The vast theatre with an open-air stage holds 5,000 people and the play, performed in two parts with a long interval for lunch, lasts nearly five hours. In addition to the vast cast of actors there is a symphony orchestra and choir. Each player has a set of three costumes, one on, one in the wash, and one drying. During the summer, every ten years, about 100 performances are given. Certainly this has become a vast commercial enterprise, but the sincerity of the performers is undoubted and to witness this play is a unique, moving experience.

In some parts of Britain Pace Egg Plays were and still are performed on Good Friday or Easter Day, which closely resembled the Christmas Mummers plays. Pace is derived from Pasche or Paschal, meaning Easter-tide. This custom still continues at Midgley in Yorkshire and the Pace Egg Play there has been performed since 1800. It is thought to be based on a 16th-century story, 'The History of Seven Champions of Christendom'.

From the events of the first Good Friday a number of superstitions have arisen. Thirteen is an unlucky number since thirteen people sat round the table at the Last Supper. Even this Christian tradition has its pagan counterpart for the Nordic myth states that Loki gate-crashed a party of twelve other Nordic gods. After that meal Loki was responsible for the death of Balder, the most popular of all the gods. The combination of Friday with thirteen is considered doubly unlucky for not only was Jesus crucified on a Friday, but Eve is supposed to have eaten the apple in the Garden of Eden on a Friday, Cain killed Abel on a Friday, and the Great Flood is reported by some scholars to have begun on a Friday.

From a legend, which told that Judas spilled the salt on the occasion of the Last Supper, arose the superstition that to spill salt is unlucky. 'Touch wood for luck', is probably an allusion to the wood of the cross on which Jesus died.

This joyous day, dear Lord, with joy, begin,
And grant that we, for whom thou didst die,
Being with thy dear blood clean, washed from sin,
May live for ever in felicity.

EDMUND SPENSER

Reference has already been made to the element of drama in the religious ceremonies of Palm Sunday and Good Friday, and the Christian Church has always found an ally in drama in presenting the faith. The first extant script demonstrating this concerns the story of Easter. A 10th-century manuscript was found in the monastery of St Gall in Switzerland which contains a short dramatisation of the visit of the three Marys to the tomb on Easter morning. It was evidently used in the form of worship. The scene is the tomb with the stone rolled away. An angel guards the place. The three Marys enter. The Angel speaks, 'Quem quaerites?' he says. 'Whom do you seek?' 'We seek the Lord,' says Mary Magdalen. 'He is not here – he is risen and gone before you.'

This short dramatisation marks the beginning of religious drama. Certainly that is the message of Easter – 'Christ is risen'.

Once again, however, one has to acknowledge that the Christian Church overlaid a festival of pre-Christian origin. Sir James Frazer in *The Golden Bough* reflects, 'We must surmise that the Easter celebration of the dead and risen Christ was grafted upon a similar celebration of the dead and risen Adonis'. From the Venerable Bede we learn that the name Easter is derived from Eastre or Eostre, the Goddess of Spring. Her month was April and this became the Paschal month of the Christian Church 'when the old festival was observed with the gladness of a new solemnity'. Mention has been made of Adonis, the God of Spring, and it is interesting to observe that Jesus is sometimes referred to as Adonai, the Supreme Being.

Easter, the feast of the Resurrection, is by far the oldest of the Christian Festivals and has been observed without fail every year since Christianity came to Britain through Cedd and Cuthbert and Augustine. In that fact alone it is unique, for all other festivals, including Christmas, have, for long or short periods, suffered eclipse.

The monks who arrived after the Conquest enriched the ceremonial, building on the short example quoted above. As the pageants grew more elaborate, instrumental and vocal music was added. Indeed, the pageants grew too splendid for some and in 1470 the properties provided for the Easter Play at St Mary Radcliffe, Bristol, included 'A new Sepulchre, well gilt with gold, an image of God rising from the sepulchre; Heaven, made of timber and dyed cloth; Hell, made of wood and iron; four pairs of Angel's wings of well painted wood; the Holy Ghost coming out of Heaven into the Sepulchre'. No mention was made of the material to be used for the Holy Ghost!

Today it is fashionable to celebrate the coming of Easter with a service at midnight with the Paschal Candle as a focal point. This candle, with its five grains of incense inserted in the form of a cross, remains lit for forty days until the Ascension, reminding us of the period of time the Risen Lord spent on earth, revealing Himself in various ways to his disciples. In the middle ages, in Durham Cathedral this candle, a monster, rose, square in section to within a man's length of the roof!

It is generally accepted that Mary entered the garden containing the tomb and made the first encounter with the risen Lord 'at the rising of the sun', and it was common at one time for people to get out into the fields before sunrise and greet the sun from the top of a nearby mound, say the Wrekin in Shropshire, or some other such eminent place. Christmas celebrations last all day with a climax towards evening, but Easter is a morning celebration.

On the table at breakfast time are Easter eggs, and with the pressures of modern commercial interests the eggs will come in all varieties of shape and content, chocolate and other confections, sometimes filled with more chocolate or an Easter gift. Even so, for many, the Easter egg that is remembered is the oldest and commonest, the coloured egg boiled in a dye. A design can easily be inscribed with a sharp steel point, just a name perhaps or a significant emblem or picture for those with artistic talent. If the eggs are meant to be kept they must be boiled very hard and they will then keep for years. There is a record that Edward I had 400 eggs boiled, stained or covered with gold leaf to be distributed among the members of his household. Red is a favourite colour, for the egg is the emblem of life and red is life's colour.

The 'Easter Bunny' has always been a favourite but the rabbit's popularity is probably due to error, for it was the hare that was sacred to Eastre. Old tales spoke of the hares running to Rome to fetch the eggs and there was in centuries past a game in which the Easter hare was said to have hidden eggs about the house and the children had to search and find them. Certainly the hare, with conspicuous outline, solitary in its attitude, seems to hold more mystery than does the rabbit. The traditional dinner for Easter is lamb, which was probably the meat at the Last Supper, while round cakes, very spicy, were specially made for this season. They were called tansy cakes or tansy pudding, for the bitter herb, tansy, was supposed to be beneficial to the digestion after eating so much fish during Lent.

Reference has been made to Pace Egg Plays performed on Good Friday or Easter Day. In many parts an activity called Pace Egg rolling takes place. Hard-boiled eggs, coloured and decorated as described above, are rolled down a slope, with prizes for the children whose eggs roll farthest. In this simple game can be seen two possible origins, the stone rolling away from the tomb of Jesus on Easter morning, or the rolling away of winter to allow new life, symbolised by the egg, to take over.

At Biddenden in Kent, anyone can apply at the Old Workhouse for a dole of bread and cheese on Easter Monday morning. This gift is in memory of Elisa and Mary Chalkhurst who were Siamese twins joined together in the back by two ligaments and who lived in the 12th century. At their death, within six hours of each other after a life of thirty-four years, they left lands to the parish, the rents from which were to be used to provide a dole of bread and cheese every Easter for the poor and needy.

At Hallaton in Leicestershire, another curious observance called 'The Hare Scramble and Bottle Kicking' takes place. The origin of the scramble is not known, but the reference to the hare marks it as pre-Christian. Now it has church blessing, for the ceremony starts in church where hare pie is cut up and distributed. Some is taken up to Hare Pie Hill to be scrambled over the ground. Then follows a boisterous game in which the youth of Hallaton struggle with the youth of neighbouring Medbourne to carry bottles or casks of beer into each other's parish, the parishes being divided by a brook. The whole performance ends with a village celebration.

Follow your spirit; and, upon this charge
Cry God for Harry! England and Saint George!
WILLIAM SHAKESPEARE

Saint George is the patron saint of England but he seems not to have achieved the popularity accorded to the patron saints of Scotland, Wales or Ireland, nor is it possible to say with certainty just who he was or what he did. There is an ancient legend given by a Byzantine named Metaphrates that George was born in the 3rd century A.D. in Cappadocia, of very noble parents who gave him a careful but strict training in the Christian faith. He chose the Roman Army for his career and rapidly rose to high military rank in the forces of the Emperor Diocletian. When he served in Persian Armenia he organised a Christian community at Urmi, and one report indicates that he visited Britain on an imperial expedition. Diocletian in later life turned against the Christians and instituted a persecution of those holding these beliefs. George sought an audience of the Emperor, to whom he made a personal confession of his faith, and tried to get him to cease his vendetta against the Christians. George was immediately arrested, tortured and put to death on 23rd April, A.D. 303.

Another account by Eusebius says that when Diocletian published the decree forbidding Christianity to be practised, George pulled down the notice from where it was posted for all to see and tore it into shreds.

George was canonised by the Church and became St George. He was not known in England until the time of the Crusades when his story was generally told. In 1098, when English and Norman soldiers were under

63

the walls of Antioch, there was a story that George appeared to lead the English and Norman forces to victory. Again, when Richard I was leading English soldiers in the Crusades against the Saracens, George is said to have appeared in order to lead them to victory. These stories were brought back to England and George was adopted as England's Patron Saint and his banner, an upright red cross on a white background, became the flag of England. The red rose, the most prolific flower of England, became its emblem. His day was declared a holiday in 1222 and Edward III founded the Order of the Garter in his name. This order is the noblest of the knightly orders of Europe. The members, limited in number, have their own chapel of St George at Windsor and the Sovereign chooses these Knights of the Garter without reference to Parliament or any minister. Fittingly, those who hold the highest ranks in the Services seem to dominate the membership.

Many legends have grown up around this figure, often involving conflict with a dragon. It is just possible to see in this conflict the pagan legend of summer defeating winter at this spring time of the year, but the origins probably lie in *The Golden Legend* by Jacobus de Voragine. In this story George, one day, found himself at Sylene in Lybia. The people were in great distress, for a neighbouring dragon was forcing the town to surrender two sheep each day for his food. Having run out of sheep, the dragon demanded two citizens in their place. When George arrived it was the turn of the King to sacrifice his daughter, who was approaching the lake where the dragon lived. She was clad in a white wedding dress. As the fearsome creature approached to take the girl, George fought the dragon and finally vanquished him by driving his spear down his throat. George then persuaded the Princess to tie her white girdle round the dragon's neck and lead him back to the town. As George reached the town the people were afraid and George promised to kill the dragon if they would become Christians. It is added that on that day 15,000 converts were made and four farm carts were needed to carry away the body of the dragon.

William Shakespeare was born, it is said, on 23rd April 1564 and died on the same day in 1616. The festival held on St George's Day in Stratford-on-Avon is one of the main celebrations of the patronal festival of St George. Visitors come from all over the world and the flags of the nations fly from flagpoles set up in the street. This is in honour of Shakespeare's birthday and it is appropriate that the memory of one of England's greatest men should be celebrated on St George's Day.

It is suitable here to mention the mummers' plays which are still performed in some parts of England, since many plots revolve round St George and variously-named enemies. These mumming plays are performed at Easter, Whitsun, All Souls and Christmas, but there is no reason why they should not find a place in the ceremonies of the English patron saint. The origins of mumming probably lie in pagan rites concerned with the eternal struggle between good and evil; winter and summer; death and resurrection. Ritual sacrifice must have been an original ingredient, for elements in contemporary mumming plays still reflect this. The Christian Church frowned on these practices and staged its own dramatic presentations in the form of miracle plays which were grouped into cycles. The scripts of presentations at York, Coventry, Wakefield and Chester survive to this day and are regularly presented.

The Bampton (Oxfordshire) Mummers' Play is

regularly presented at Christmas, and so the central character or compere is Father Christmas, but another character could be found to present the play at other times of the year. The players process from one hostelry to another, presenting their 20-minute play, being suitably refreshed and passing on. Possibly the words are changed to accommodate reference to members of the audience, whose idiosyncracies are known to all present.

Father Christmas introduces the characters who include St George, the Doctor, a Turk, Robin Hood, Little John, the Royal Apprusia King, a soldier bold, Jack Finney and Tom the Tinker. The plot involves fights between St George and the Turk and St George and the Prussian. Wounds are healed miraculously and dead characters are brought to life.

One of the most important festivals in the Buddhist calendar takes place at the time of the full moon day of the month of Vesakha, corresponding to the month of May in the Christian calendar. This festival celebrates the birth day and death day of Buddha as well as what is known as his enlightenment.

Buddha was born in 560 B.C., the son of a ruler of a small kingdom in northern India called Sakya. When his mother, Queen Mahamaya, knew that she was to have this baby, in compliance with custom she made her way to her parents' home, travelling in a decorated palanquin, which is a covered litter carried by four bearers. On the way, Queen Mahamaya halted to rest in the shade of a Sala tree where, as it happened, she had her baby. There was no point in going on, so the Queen went back to Sakya with the prince, her son. He was called Siddhartha, meaning 'wish fulfilled'. The prince was born on the full moon day of Vesakha.

At that time the civilization in northern India was relatively civilized and although the word 'Hindu' did not exist, the caste system was already well founded with Brahmins as priests and tutors of religion, Kshatriyas as the warrior ruling class, Vaishyas as merchants, and Sudras working as labourers and servants. Kala Devala, a wise man, was the first to prophesy that the boy would be exceptional. He smiled when he forecast that the prince would be 'enlightened' and wept at the thought that he would not live to see it. Brahmins who examined the boy declared that he would in due course see four signs which would impel him to renounce his home and the world and go out to seek enlightenment.

His mother died when he was only seven days old,

but he was cared for by an aunt who also married his father. There are many stories about the young prince's compassion and his search for answers to the many questions about human existence. He emphasised in his own life the importance of self-denial and meditation.

The King was still concerned about losing the boy and asked the Brahmins to tell him what were the four signs which would change the boy's life. They said he would give up the life of a prince and become a religious leader or Buddha if he saw an old man, a sick man, a dead man and finally an ascetic, that is, someone who gives up all wordly things and imposes on himself a life of complete self-denial.

In spite of all the king's efforts to keep from Siddhartha all signs of age, illness, death and poverty, in due course the prince saw them all. He was appalled to see age, illness and death, but was impressed by the serenity of one who had given up all the material things in life in order to meditate and seek an answer through prayer and self-examination.

Soon after, his wife, for he had by now married a princess in accordance with his father's wishes, gave birth to a son. Far from being delighted, Siddhartha only saw this as an additional bondage to worldly things.

Siddhartha made up his mind to leave the life of a prince and, without even seeing his son, taking only his horse Kanthaka and a servant named Channa, set off for the frontier of his homeland, the river Anoma. There he cut off his long hair with his sword, changed his royal clothing for the orange robe of a beggar and, taking up a begging bowl, said 'goodbye' to his servant and his horse. At first the horse would not leave him and even when Channa did persuade him to leave his master to return to the palace, the horse stopped to turn to his master again. Later, the horse died of a broken heart.

Siddhartha gave up his name and preferred to be addressed by his family name, Gautama. He joined five other ascetics and this group enrolled under a leader or guru called Alara Kalama who quickly realised that Gautama had the ability to achieve supreme levels of meditation.

Soon the pupils were in advance of the guru and so set out to found their own hermitage. Gautama strove to see how far he could punish his own body in order to achieve deeper spirituality. He cut down his food until he lived on plant roots and leaves, he held his breath for long periods until it seemed his head would burst. In summer he stayed out in the burning sun, in winter he bathed in icy water. After six years he began to eat again and regained his former health.

Then came the event in his life, the enlightenment experience. He resolved to sit cross-legged at the foot of the Bodhi tree in a trance from which he emerged with knowledge of former existences, the power to see passing away and rebirth, and full knowledge of all evil. In some ways the experience corresponds with the forty days Jesus spent in the wilderness. Some accounts say that Gautama spent forty-nine days in meditation.

He emerged as the day of the full moon of Vesakha was setting. He became known as 'The Fully Enlightened One' or Buddha. The Buddha was then thirty-five years old. His teaching ministry lasted forty-five years and he died like any other man in a relatively insignificant place, Kusinara. His death occurred on the day of the full moon of Vesakha.

After his cremation his relics were distributed for his followers to venerate and these provide a means of communication between the devotee and the Buddha.

Very little has been written on the subject of festivals and ceremonies in Buddhism, for most are very local and, if written up at all, would be in the language of the area concerned. The festival of Vesakha (Wesak is a western corruption of the name) brings Buddhists together in the Vihara, corresponding to the Temple, where they are led by Priests or Lamas in meditation and discourses.

Buddhists have no domestic ceremonies, although families come to the Temple for a blessing from the monks or bhikkus when a child is born. After a civil registration of a wedding, Buddhists go to the Temple for a religious ceremony and elaborate rituals are followed on the occasion of funerals and memorial services.

May Day can safely be included among the pagan festivals which later established religious associations. Its origin is disputed but most probably it stems from the Roman festival to Maia, mother of Mercury, in whose honour sacrifices were made on the first day of her month, accompanied by considerable merry-making. In *The Golden Bough*, J. C. Frazer links the celebrations on May Day, especially the prominence given to the Maypole, with the beneficent qualities ascribed to tree spirits and indicates that May Day celebrations are relics of pagan tree worship.

In medieval and Tudor England, May Day was a great public holiday when most villages arranged processions, with everyone carrying green boughs of sycamore and hawthorn. Pride of place in the procession would be given to a young tree, 12 to 15 feet (3.6 to 4.6m) high, bedecked with garlands of flowers and ribbons. The tree would be stripped of its branches with the exception of the topmost bough, whose leaves would be left to show signs of life, new life at this beginning of summer. Sometimes the tree would be completely stripped so that the top could be decorated by attaching floral garlands in the shape of crowns, cowslip balls, floral globes or versions of the Christmas kissing boughs. In some villages the decoration took the form of two intersecting circles of garlands or flowers, similar to some modern Christmas decorations, bound with ribbons which spiralled down the tree. There are records of traditions in which blown wild birds' eggs were attached to the top of the tree or, on occasion, dolls which may have originally represented Flora, the Roman goddess of flowers. More recently the reverence is directed towards the Mother of Jesus, and May is recognised by the Church as the month of Mary.

While the Maypole was the centre of attention on this day, the fun and games which were occasioned by the May Day holiday were greatly frowned on by the Church for their excesses. It was this aspect of May Day that occasioned the comment by Philip Stubbes in *The Anatomie of Abuses*: 'All the young men and maids, old men and wives, run gadding over night to the woods, groves and hills, where they spend all the night in pleasant pastimes. In the morning they return bringing with them birch and branches of trees, to deck their assemblies. There is a great Lord over their pastimes, namely Satan, Prince of Hell. The chiefest jewel they bring is their Maypole. They have twentie or fortie oxen, every one having a sweet nosegay of flowers on the tip of his horns, and these oxen drag the Maypole (this stinking idol, rather) which is covered with flowers and herbs, bound round with string from top to bottom and painted with variable colours.'

Henry VIII went Maying on many occasions and it is reported that he went early one May Day with Catherine of Aragon, from Greenwich to Shooters Hill and watched a company of yeomen dressed in green with their chieftain who was called Robin Hood, a character that represented Old England. Henry stayed to witness their archery contest. May Day was certainly an energetic festival, starting as it did the previous evening, including dancing and games throughout the day and ending with bonfires, known in some parts as Beltone fires, for Beltone was the name given by the Celts for their fire festival of May 1st.

The Puritans frowned on all these activities and were dismayed when James I perpetuated the legality of setting up Maypoles. Once in power the rebel Parliament forbade the celebrations of May Day and Christmas Day. Both were thought to encourage excesses and wantonness. The Puritan order indicates that some Maypoles had been set up as permanent fixtures. A Maypole at Lostock is recorded as early as the reign of King John and others were set up in London as lofty as church towers, painted in spiral bands like vertical barbers' poles, dressed on May Day with garlands of flowers, ribbons and flags. One church, somewhat dwarfed by such a Maypole, was known as St Andrew Undershaft, the shaft being the Maypole.

Inevitably, with the Restoration of the Stuarts came the restoration of Maypoles. Samuel Pepys declared that the first May Day in King Charles' reign was 'The happiest May Day that hath been many a year in England'. A great Maypole, over 130 feet (40m) high, was set up in the Strand. So vast was this pole, made in two parts, that it was floated along the river to where Scotland Yard now stands and carried in procession along White-hall, accompanied by bands and multitudes of people. Twelve seamen took four hours to set it up with block and tackle.

To some extent, however, the Restoration limited the recognition and observance of May Day, for it was replaced by Oak Apple Day, May 29th, by coincidence the date both of Charles II's birthday and of his return to the throne. The name given to this day refers to the incident at Boscobel House when Charles, after his defeat at nearby Worcester, hid in the branches of an oak tree while Cromwell's soldiers searched the house and the area around it. After this adventure Charles escaped to France. For some time sprigs of oak were worn to commemorate the day.

By the 18th century the May Day festival had largely disappeared, and in 1717 the highest permanent Maypole was removed to Wanstead Park in Essex where Sir Isaac Newton used it to support the most modern and powerful telescope in the world. But that is not the end of May Day.

The 20th century has seen a renewal of interest in it. In Primary Schools, Maypoles have never quite lost their fascination. Intricate dances have evolved using the coloured ribbons in patterns formed by the steps of the dancers, round and about each other. We owe this infusion of new life to the festival to Tennyson, William Morris and Ruskin, who made it a children's day. Often the May Day ceremony is accompanied by the crowning of a May Queen, sometimes with references to the Queen of Heaven, Mary, Our Lord's Mother, whose month it is.

On the secular side of this curious celebration day, in 1889 it was chosen by the Congress of the Second International as Labour Day – a day of the working people with little or no reference to religious matters. In England, particularly in the industrial north, it is once more a day of fairs, music, processions and dancing with the occasional suitable political reference in the presence of distinguished Socialist statesmen. May 1st may well become a public bank holiday. So, through the centuries, this festival, pagan or religious, has been and is celebrated in England.

At Tissington in Derbyshire, bright, elaborate pictures are placed in well heads on May morning and a little thanksgiving service is held. The pictures are of religious subjects and are made from flower petals, mosses, lichen and berries stuck in wet clay. In grains of rice above the picture are written the words, 'Praise the Lord'. At

Helston, where in recent times the festival has been transferred to May 8th, there is a general holiday with the much-reported Furry Dance. Quite early the houses are decorated and by seven o'clock there is dancing in the streets. The band leads the dancing to bring in the 'Summer'.

On May morning a hymn is sung at sunrise on the top of the Bargate in Southampton, but the best-known event of this kind to take place on May morning is the singing of carols from the top of Magdalen College Tower in Oxford at six o'clock a.m. Unfortunately the custom of singing from Magdalen College Tower has been broken by the need to restore the stonework, so that from 1977 until 1982, while this work is going on, the choir sings from the neighbouring Fellows Tower at Magdalen. This does not in any way inhibit the ceremony which bears many reflections of the medieval May morning. There are many all-night parties held which end up in 'the High' just before dawn, with champagne and other liquids poured liberally. These formally-dressed groups mingle with others in extravagantly informal and even bizarre dress. From Magdalen bridge down to Carfax, the High Street is packed with a crowd estimated in recent years at about 15,000. In modern times with the aid of amplifiers they all hear with ease, first the clock bell striking six, and then the magnificent singing of 'Te deum patrem colimus'. For this and the following madrigal, 'Now is the month of Maying', the listeners are silent, but as soon as the madrigal ends, a riot of activity ensues. Groups of Morris dancers attract spectators in all parts of the town. Musicians, offering a variety of styles, set up on stone steps, tops of walls or any other suitable platform. The onlooker can choose anything from joining in 'modern' dancing or listening to Purcell. Meanwhile the bells from towers all over the city ring out. Not far away in Cowley, children bring bunches of flowers to church and at Chorlton a wooden cross above the screen is decorated for May morning.

So, another pagan festival is taken over and given a Christian significance. In the Oxford Book of Carols are several May Songs, the most attractive of them being the Furry Day Carol (Furry is derived from Feria, holy day and thence, holiday).

> Remember us poor Mayers all!
> And thus do we begin – a
> To lead our lives in righteousness
> Or else we die in sin – a.

These days derive their name from the Latin word 'rogare' meaning to beseech, or ask for. They were for long associated with the chanting of litanies or petitions, in processions around the church. In A.D. 511 the Council of Orleans declared that the three days before Ascension Day (commemorating the Ascension of Jesus Christ) should be holidays and used for prayer and fasting. The processions tended to go on outside the church and indeed to circle the parish, with prayers and petitions largely concerned with the success of the crops for the coming harvest. The processions halted at various points in the parish and nearly always included a 'Gospel Oak', where prayers were recited. A modern survival of these processions is the custom in many parishes of 'beating the bounds'. Why this custom is associated with Rogationtide is difficult to understand but one theory is that the festival in early days of the Christian Church coincided with two former Roman festivals of Terminalia and Ambarvalia. The statue of Terminus was not in the form of a man, but took the shape of a wooden post or boundary stone marking the end of one property and the beginning of another. Ambarvalia, about the same time of the year, involved processions around the fields, the people carrying sticks to beat the ground in order to drive away the winter.

A combination of the Christian Rogation ceremonial, with the beating of sticks of Ambarvalia and the boundary stone of Terminalia, may reasonably be said to account for the quaint ceremony performed in many parishes at Rogationtide of 'beating the bounds'.

A procession forms up at the church with the priest in front followed by someone bearing the ceremonial crucifix. This is followed by the choir, dressed in gowns and white surplices, and a crowd of parishioners, including schoolboys with their masters. Most of them carry willow wands, peeled white and sometimes topped with small bunches of wild flowers. At well-known points along the boundary of the parish, a gate, a tree, a bridge, or a road crossing, the company gather round and join in prayers asking God for good seasonable weather, good crops and a successful harvest. At some points food and drink will be waiting. At the Gospel Oak, or at some prominent landmark, the wand bearers set about beating the landmark, then transfer their attention to one of the boys who offers himself with some reluctance to be beaten. The victim will be rolled in the grass or briars and bumped against the landmark. The boy who suffers in this way is rewarded with an appropriate coin. Since maps in those days were largely unknown and those that existed were inaccurate, this was probably a sensible way of marking the boundaries. If later there should be a dispute between parishes, somebody would come forward with certainty and assert, 'That's where I was beaten'.

The custom was less popular in the 19th century, but recently there has been a revival even if the procession now visits, not fields, gates and barns, but streets and factories.

At St Clement Danes in London, the procession with clergy and choir follows the mace, borne by the beadle. The schoolboys carry willow wands topped with ribbons or flowers. The boundary stones are beaten even though, to beat the southern boundary which lies along the River Thames, the procession takes to boats.

SHOVUOS (PENTECOST)
(*Jewish Festival*)

> *Even unto the morrow after the seventh sabbath shall
> ye number fifty days.*
>
> Leviticus 23.xvi

Shovuos, the festival of weeks, comes seven weeks or fifty days (hence the name Pentecost) after the Passover. The festival originally celebrated the gathering of the barley harvest, seven weeks after the harvesting of the wheat. It was, therefore, a thanksgiving and a harvest festival and was first observed after the Jews had settled in Palestine and had become a farming community. In its earliest days Shovuos was a minor festival but it gained greater importance when it was observed as the festival of the Torah, which is the Hebrew Law given to the Jews by God on Mount Sinai. The Bible story tells that the Jews entered the desert of Sinai in the third month after leaving Egypt. Through this association, Shovuos achieved importance as one of the great Jewish festivals. Much later, in the 19th century, the festival became even more important when it was recognised as the day of confirmation, when young people of thirteen years of age were confirmed in the faith at a special ceremony. Previously only boys were permitted to go through this ceremony known as Bar Mitzvah, but now both boys and girls are confirmed when they are thirteen. All this makes the festival of Shovuos very significant.

Inevitably, the festival has a Christian significance, for it was at Pentecost that the disciples of Jesus suddenly found they had the courage to go out and tell the whole world of their belief, and in later days this festival called Whitsun in the Christian calendar, became a popular day for baptism and confirmation in the Christian faith.

Shovuos is a summer festival and Jewish homes are decorated in green while the food is largely made up of dairy dishes. A popular dish is fried blintzes, cheese rolled in dough.

In schools the children are told the story of Ruth which reminds them of the agricultural beginnings of Jewish custom and history and also turns their thoughts to Bethlehem and David, the great Jewish King-hero. The story begins in Bethlehem in a time of hardship and famine. A farmer named Elimelech with his wife, Naomi, and their two sons, decided to move to another country, Moab, to find better fortune there. Sadly, Elimelech died and the two boys looked after Naomi. In due course the boys married, the elder of them to a Moabite girl, Ruth. Naomi found happiness with her two daughters-in-law and her sons and they prospered for ten years. Then, tragically, the two sons were killed in an accident and Naomi, now very lonely, decided to go back to Bethlehem. Ruth asked to go with her with the words:

> Wherever you go, I will go,
> Wherever you live, I will live.
> Your people shall be my people
> and your God, my God.

They went back to Bethlehem together, to find the situation very different from that of ten years before. The famine was over and the harvests good. Even so, the two women were poor and at harvest time Ruth went into the fields to gather corn that had been left by the reapers. The owner of the field, Boaz, saw her, fell in love with her, and married her. They had a son called Obed, who in due course was grandfather to David.

Christians find this story of great significance for Jesus was eventually to be born in Bethlehem, a descendant of David.

The Bar Mitzvah (boys) and Bat Mitzvah (girls) ceremonies mark the occasion when the young Jew reaches religious and legal maturity. It is the occasion for ceremonial in the synagogue and celebration in the home. The young boy is called upon to read the Torah or Law, and a great party is given by the parents to which even distant relatives are invited. A high point in the festivity is a speech by the young person in which thanks to the parents for their love and concern are expressed.

WHIT-SUNDAY   *Seven weeks after Easter Sunday*

The world is charged with the grandeur of God,
It will flame out, like shining shook foil.
GERALD MANLEY HOPKINS

Of the three major festivals in the Christian calendar, in general, Whitsun is the least regarded and celebrated by people in England. Christmas celebrates the birth of a child in a stable, Easter celebrates the Risen Lord. These events are not difficult to imagine and each come at an appropriate season of the year for celebration, for Christmas brightens mid-winter and Easter heralds the spring.

The coming of the Holy Spirit to revitalise the apostles and, through them, the whole church, is much more difficult to picture and to some extent in former days Whitsun was upstaged by May Day. Indeed, Whitsun no longer claims a general holiday in its own right in Britain, but can only be celebrated with a general holiday on the Monday if an accident of the calendar permits Whit-Sunday to fall on the day before the Spring Bank Holiday.

After the events of Easter Day, the disciples of Jesus were comforted and encouraged for forty days by his appearances before them. The apostles were still looking for 'a kingdom of Christ' and needed the presence of the King. However, Jesus told them that it was not for them to know how this kingdom would be achieved, but he would always be with them and they would be inspired by the Holy Spirit. Then, forty days after Easter, he went from their sight. This event is remembered by the Church as Ascension Day. Ten days later the apostles (now made up to twelve by the appointment of Matthias to take the place of Judas Iscariot) were together to celebrate the Jewish festival of the fifty days, Pentecost. As they talked, fearful of what was to happen to them, a power came to them, in a moment of time, which they all experienced, and which, sweeping away their fears, emboldened them to go out to the crowds and inspired them to preach the gospel of Jesus Christ in such a way that all the crowds, collected together from many lands, could understand what they were excited about. The missionary work of the Christian church had begun its endless life, which was to bring death in cruel forms to some of the twelve. The name of the festival is derived from the Saxon 'Hirita Surnondseg' or 'White Sunday'. It was customary for many baptisms to take place on this day and the onlookers were impressed by the spectacle of so many people gathered together in white clothing.

Today most ceremonies which take place at Ascension or Whitsuntide seem to have little reference to the events of the first Whitsun described above and may owe their origins to pagan custom, although the Church has changed the emphasis. The pagan cult of well worship and veneration of water spirits was one of the most difficult features to eradicate. To this day there is an affection for wishing wells, and throwing coins in a fountain or well-head is still a popular custom from which many charities gain income. It is still not unknown for sick people's relatives to take a rag or cloth to a well and hang it nearby for its curative powers.

The most colourful ceremony which takes place in modern times, largely at Ascensiontide, is Well Dressing, very popular in the Midlands and Peak District. This has become an art form in its own right with origins in the Dark Ages and floral pictures up to ten feet (3m) in height are set up at springs and well-heads. Tissington, Buxton and Wirksworth are notable for the size and beauty of their well dressings. The scenes depicted are biblical and the pictures are constructed entirely from natural materials, pebbles, flowers and flower petals, leaves, moss and pieces of crystalline rock.

At Tissington on Ascension Day, after morning service, the clergy and choir process to each of five local wells, where the enormous floral pictures are blessed.

Whitsun celebrations, however, apart from the services of the church, justified by Pentecost, have nevertheless been secular in character.

The Whitsun Ale was a sort of parish carousel vaguely linked with the Agapae or Love Feasts of the early Church when the rich ate with the poor and shared their food. The churchwardens arranged the event and provided the beer which was sold, with all profits going to the poor.

In more recent times the church ale led to the old village benefit clubs of the 19th century which did little to benefit their members, and these in turn gave way to soundly-conducted benefit societies. More than anything today, Whitsun is the time of the Morris Dance, and the popularity of this movement, encouraged by the English Folk Dance Society and intense research on the part of enthusiasts, has never been greater.

One of the strongholds of the Morris Dance is at Bampton in Oxfordshire where Mr Arnold Woodley trains his enthusiastic team, with no shortage of reserves and would-be dancers, throughout the year. Quite recently he was called upon to train the dancers of the Royal Ballet at Covent Garden when they included 'The Morris Men' in their repertoire. On Whit-Monday (now, alas, leaving pride of place to Spring Bank Holiday) the team begin their day dancing outside the Old People's Flats in Bampton at 9 o'clock in the morning and the sun sets on their last performances somewhere in the village, the itinerary having included all the parts of Bampton with suitable breaks for refreshment.

The Morris is the English version of the Morisca or Moorish Dance which began as a ritualistic form of battle mime and the element of conflict or confrontation still persists in the various dances. Possibly the Crusaders were intrigued by witnessing these dances during their travels and brought them back to England. Occasionally, the Morris is a solo jig danced like the Scottish sword dance between two crossed swords, but generally it is performed longwise by a team of six men with accompanying traditional characters. In the north-east of England the team can be made up of ten men. 'The Squire' is the leader or trainer, 'The Fiddler' is the accompanist, superseding first the bagpipes and later the drum and fife. The associated characters are 'The Fool', 'The Cake Carrier' and 'The Treasury'. The Fool cavorts in and out with primitive humour and whacks any dancers who happen to make a false step or movement with a bullock's bladder. The Cake Carrier attends with a spiced fruit cake borne aloft which has a sword through the centre pointing upwards, and is decorated with flowers at the point of the sword. Girls try to snatch pieces of the cake because it is said to bring luck and to increase fertility. Taking some of the cake is made difficult by the sharp, serrated edge of the cake tin. Other attendants hold baskets for the 'Treasury', the collection taken in payment for the efforts of the dancers.

The steps are precise and are danced with a rude vigour. They are called capers, springs, kicks, cross-steps, side-steps, straddle, swings and high jumps. The last of these steps are accompanied by loud shouts.

The figures vary and include Processional, Stick dancing, Handkerchief dancing, Corner dancing and Morris Off, a circular prelude to the exit. The formations of the dances include longways figures, corners, cross-overs, heys and circles. The dancers' costumes have changed somewhat but still retain the original characteristics.

At Bampton the costume comprises white shirt and trousers, blue tie with crest, black shoes, decorated bell pads attached to the lower leg, black bowler hat with floral decoration and ribbons of yellow, red and blue attached to the hat, with red and yellow ribbons flowing from the arms of the shirt. All the dancers carry a white handkerchief in each hand.

The melodies are quaint and original, handed down from Fiddler to Fiddler, many of whom cannot read music at all. The Morris Dancing at Bampton has gone on for 600 years at least. Among the dancing tunes are 'Old Tom of Oxford', 'The Nutting Girl', 'Jogging to the Fair', and 'The Forester'. Most of the tunes have words, for example:

To the tune of Green Garters

First for the stockings and then for the shoes,
And then for the bonny green garters;
A pair for me and a pair for you,
And a pair for they that comes after.

This dance, called by the Bampton dancers 'Greenies', is their 'Morris Off' and, as the dancers circle at the end of the dance, the leader precedes the line of dancers on to the next stopping place.

Bampton has another pretty Whitsun custom, for the children make floral decorations like the Christmas or

Kissing Bower, two intertwined circles of flowers, and these are carried, three or more at a time, on wooden staffs from house to house. The children knock at the door and say 'Please to see the garlands' and expect a coin or two for their trouble. These garlands have to be made from wild flowers and the whole family helps in making them. The art is thus handed down from grand-mother to the younger generation. Some time during the day the children bring all the garlands to the village centre and the children whose garlands are judged best receive prizes.

In the churchwarden's accounts in the 15th, 16th and 17th centuries there are many entries of payments made for such items as a hobby horse, dancing bells, beer, and even payment for the dancing. Morris men were con-sidered lawful entertainers, as they are to this day.

Not everyone was in favour as is evidenced by this extract from Philip Stubbes' *Anatomie of Abuses*, written in the 16th century:

> As though they were not bawdie and gawdie enough they bedecke themselves with scarfs, ribbons and laces, they tie about either leg twenty or forty bells, with rich handkerchieves in their hands and sometimes lay a crosse over their shoulders and necks borrowed of their pretty Mopsies and Bessies. Then they march, this heathen company, towards the churchyard, their pipers piping, their drummers drumming, their bells jingling and their handkerchiefs swinging about their heads like madmen.

Perhaps Philip Stubbes would have approved of the cycles of miracle plays which are sometimes performed at Whitsuntide at Chester, Wakefield and Coventry. The miracle plays evolved from early forms of religious

87

drama which began to develop boisterous and sometimes bawdy features which were not considered seemly in church.

The trade guilds took over and presented scenes on 'pageants' or moving stages which processed round the town so that the various groups of onlookers stayed in one place while a great number of pageants rolled in front of them to present one scene from the total 'miracle' play. The stories were basically biblical, but freed from the censorship of the church, became popular for the scenic effects achieved by the productions and the homespun humour introduced. In time, some of them were scripted and are now achieving a new life by the popularity of modern productions.

Kingsteignton, near Newton Abbot in Devonshire, celebrates Whitsun with a Monday Ram Fair. The origins of the Ram Fair are obscure but seem to derive from a sacrifice of thanks for a spring of water which continued to flow during a severe drought and continues to flow to this day. One story looks back to pagan origins when the miraculous flow began during a drought as a result of the sacrifice of a ram. Another claim is that the well sprang up as a result of prayer during a drought when all the wells in the area ran dry. Whatever the origin, a ram decorated with ribbons and garlands is ceremonially processed through the streets and later killed, roasted for a barbecue and slices sold to onlookers. The original price per slice was one penny, but as with all things, inflation has increased this. The spot is clearly marked on Ordnance Survey maps as Well Head.

INDEPENDENCE DAY
(UNITED STATES OF AMERICA)

July 4th

> *We hold these truths to be self-evident;*
> *that all men are created equal; that they*
> *are endowed by their Creator with*
> *certain inalienable rights; that among*
> *these are life, liberty and the pursuit of*
> *happiness.*
>
> THOMAS JEFFERSON
> Declaration of Independence,
> 4th July, 1776.

The fourth of July is probably the most important day in the national history of the United States of America. It is an important date in British history, too. On 4th July, 1776, Britain lost a great part of what was then her Empire, a part she might have held longer, although it is very doubtful whether she could have held America for ever.

The seeds of Independence were sown in 1608 when John Smith founded the state of Virginia, after earlier unsuccessful attempts at settlement with adventure and material gains as motives. The move towards Independence had further impetus when the Pilgrim Fathers sailed in *The Mayflower* in 1620 to seek a country where they could practise their own chosen way of life which had been impossible in the Mother country. From these beginnings grew five separate colonies followed by the foundation of Maryland in 1633 by Roman Catholics who also found England at that time intolerant of their religion. Other colonists followed from Ireland, France and Holland, as well as from England, until by the reign of George III there were thirteen colonies strung along the Atlantic coast of North America.

The colonists considered themselves subjects of the King of England and at that time there was little conscious urge to become independent, but as the years went by their dislike of being governed from London increased, particularly since they were not permitted to have representatives in Parliament. Even more did they feel growing resentment against paying taxes to this distant Government, thousands of miles away and several weeks away by sea voyage. The English people themselves had, in the previous century, fought the King in a Civil War over similar tax grievances. On that occasion the Sovereign had lost the cause and his head. The colonies had their own assemblies, it is true, but governors were appointed from England and trade laws and regulations were imposed with high duties and restrictions. The American colonists protested with the slogan 'No taxation without representation', but George III's government made no concessions, regarding the colonies as existing to support and benefit England.

British rule was enforced by troops who as early as 1770 had been forced to open fire on demonstrators in Boston, but in 1773 the incident happened that has caught the imagination ever since. This was the 'Boston Tea Party'. Lord North, the English Prime Minister, bowed to the storm a little by repealing many of the duties but insisted on maintaining a tax of threepence on every pound of tea entering America. A committee was formed in Boston which published statements intended to incite action against the tea tax. Samuel Adams, a Massachusetts politician, endeavoured to unite all thirteen states into an American Commonwealth.

Tea ships were due to arrive at Boston and when *The Dartmouth* arrived, although its captain promised not to land the tea, the Boston people were still suspicious.

Eventually the cargo of *The Dartmouth*, all but the tea, was landed, but the ship was refused clearance by the Controller of Customs, and so could not put to sea.

While a meeting between Samuel Adams and the captain of *The Dartmouth* was in progress there were wild shouts and a body of forty or fifty men, dressed as Mohawk Indians, raced down to the harbour and boarded the ship in question. In about three hours, 340 chests of tea had been tipped into the harbour. There was no riot or disorder and as soon as the tea was disposed of the 'Mohawk Indians' retired and the town was quiet. The harbour water was black with tea. A message was sent from Boston to New York and Philadelphia. The horseman who took the message was Paul Revere.

> So through the night rode Paul Revere;
> And so through the night went his cry of alarm
> To every Middlesex village and farm
> A cry of defiance and not of fear.   *Longfellow*

This incident, however, was a turning point, for although there were men of goodwill on both sides, the general response was to take sides and prepare for conflict. The British Parliament passed repressive acts and the colonists prepared a Declaration of Rights. Even so, not all the colonists wanted to break with England, but the militant action on the part of the British Government tended to unite the Americans. A Continental Congress was held in Philadelphia setting out the demands of the colonists.

The first clash of arms came at Lexington in April 1775, as a result of which the American colonists formed their own militia with George Washington as its first Commander in Chief. Other officers were chosen and soldiers known as 'minute men' were enrolled. They were so called because they could leave their jobs to fight at a minute's notice.

The next military encounter was at Breeds Hill across the river from Boston which was only just won by the British at great cost. This battle is more generally known as 'Bunkers Hill', although that was a neighbouring height on which no fighting really took place.

Both sides met difficulties. Washington found some of his troops not amenable to discipline, while George III found incompetence in his generals and a reluctance to enlist among his subjects. So much so that, to continue the war, Britain had to enlist about 18,000 German mercenaries. This enlistment of foreign soldiers so incensed the Americans that they drew up their Declaration of Independence. The Continental Congress met once more in the State House at Philadelphia. John Trumbull's famous painting now hanging in the Capitol depicts the delegates in knee-breeches and stockings in the hall hung with crossed banners, the table strewn with documents.

The vote for independence came on 2nd July, 1776 and Thomas Jefferson, a Virginian planter, undertook to draft the document. This was adopted on July 4th, and the words at the head of this chapter began the document which saw the birth of the United States of America. The phrases demonstrate Jefferson's intellectual and philosophic mind, as well as reflecting his Welsh ancestry. Jefferson's father came from Glynceiriog in North Wales.

This was not the end of the war, for it dragged on for another five years, largely due to the personal reluctance of George III to give up, but also because on the American side there were some who would have liked a compromise solution. At one point an American general,

Benedict Arnold, was prepared to betray to the British all the forts round the Hudson river.

France and Spain gave assistance to the Americans and by the Treaty of Paris 1782, the Independence of America was recognised. The compliments paid by the British Government to the Americans, and those passed over by the American representatives to George III, enabled the break to be made without rancour and now Britons and Americans together can celebrate the Fourth of July with great good humour and friendship.

Independence Day festivities are usually held outdoors with parades, barbecues and picnics. Possibly the cere-monies and celebrations are more enthusiastic in the small towns where community spirit is more intense. The flag of the United States is displayed everywhere, and in schools the theme of Independence runs through projects and pageants. Most families attend church services on the previous Sunday and speeches by mayors or senators are featured in the general assemblies. Business concerns hold Independence parties and picnics where local bands and majorettes parade. After the barbecues, with hot dogs and hamburgers, the day ends with a bang – monster firework displays.

The mood of the day is one of patriotism but also one of reconciliation, for out of the disagreement and conflict has grown a great warmth and friendship between Great Britain and the United States of America.

RAKSHABANDHAN *July/August*
(*Hindu Festival*)

This is a festival for brothers and sisters in the family. It falls on the day of the full moon in the Hindu month Shravana, which generally coincides with July or August. Sisters tie Rakshabandhan (meaning a tie for security), which is popularly called Rakhi, on their brothers' wrists. Rakhi is made from coloured cotton or silk threads with a little decoration showing at the wrist. Rakhi obliges the brothers to care for the safety of their sisters. The brother then returns the compliment with a present to the sister. This present can take the form of cash or an article of clothing or jewellery. The sister also puts a special mark of vermilion powder on the brother's forehead, a special symbol for success and victory, and then gives a gift of sweetmeats to her brother.

This festival is also a religious occasion when Hindus give of their charity to Brahmins and if possible go to bathe in the holy waters of the Ganges or some other local sacred river, or in coastal waters. In the coastal regions which grow coconuts in abundance, there is also a custom of offering the sea whole coconuts. In one such region, viz. Maharashtra (Bombay), the festival is actually known as Narali Purnima (Full Moon day of Coconuts).

The Rakhi festival has a special appeal in India which extends to other non-Hindu communities. One story tells how, during the Muslim rule, a beautiful Hindu Queen called Padmini sought protection from the Mughal Emperor by sending him a Rakhi. When Padmini was threatened by another Muslim King who had determined to marry her when he saw her reflection in a mirror, the Queen was defended against this invasion by the Mughal Emperor in response to her Rakhi. To this day Rakhi from a woman to a man is honoured even when the man is not a Hindu.

However, the important thing to remember about Rakhi is that it is a family celebration between brother and sister and also between cousins.

RAMADAN   *Ninth month in Muslim Calendar*
(*Muslim Festival*)

Muslims, followers of the religion of Islam, have a duty to try to make a pilgrimage to Mecca at least once during their lives, but this can be undertaken by only a small proportion of the faithful. The duty of fasting through the month of Ramadan, however, affects the life of every one of those who follow the faith of Islam.

Muhammad was well aware of the Jewish and Christian custom of fasting, or of abstinence, at certain times in order to emphasise solemn occasions or prepare for the great festivals. Following this example, inspired by God, he ordered Muslims to observe a month-long fast during Ramadan. Strictly, the believer was to have nothing to eat or drink from the time of sunrise to the hour of sunset for a period of twenty-eight days. This has come to be the most important religious act of the Muslims.

The timing of the fast has changed several times, but now Ramadan is established so as to include the 'Lailat al Qadr', 'The Night of Power', which celebrates the night in which the Prophet Muhammad first received the message from God communicated by the Angel Gabriel. Muhammad was forty years old, and from then on he recorded his inspirations which comprise the holy book of Islam, *The Koran*. The communication of the *Koran* to Prophet Muhammad continued until his death, twenty-three years later.

The first verses recited to the Prophet by Gabriel were:
> Read, in the name of thy Sustainer who created
>   Man,
> Thy Sustainer is the Most Bountiful One
> Who taught the use of the pen –
> Taught Man that which he knew not.

The observance of the fast is very strict and is not only concerned with avoiding food and drink. It demands that the believer avoids thinking of anything which might distract him from thinking about God. The believer must avoid lies, back-biting, slander, swearing, indecent or dishonest talk. The fast is not obligatory to the ordinary believer on every day of the month. Certain days are considered better days, but the Muslim observes the fast as well as he is able without making himself ill or depressed. Alternate days or one day in three is the common pattern.

Reading the *Koran* is an important part of the fast, and some Muslims read a thirtieth part of the book each day, thus reading the whole of it during Ramadan. It is not such a big book as the Christian *Bible*, or even the Jewish Testament, containing only some 300 pages in all.

The arrival of the new moon announcing the end of the month of Ramadan is awaited with great excitement. This is a party occasion with visits to the mosque, friends' houses and exchange of greetings in the streets. One of the most common forms of greeting is 'If I have done you any wrong, please forgive me'. The festival that follows Ramadan lasts three days and is known as 'The feast of the breaking of the fast'. Another feature of the ending of the fast is its combination with a festival of remembrance of the dead. Families visit the graves and tombs of relatives.

It is difficult for a western mind to appreciate the *Koran*, for in translation the beauty and musical quality is lost. Essentially the *Koran* is meant to be listened to as it is read aloud. Christians may be surprised to find many references to characters in the Old and New Testaments such as Noah, Joseph, Abraham, Moses, David, Solomon, Mary and Jesus. There is ample evidence of prophetic inspiration common to Muslim, Jew, and Christian. Mary, the mother of Jesus, stands highest among the women honoured in the *Koran* and the story of the visit of the angel to tell Mary that she was to bear the child Jesus is told more than once.

In the chapter named after Mary, the story begins with these words:

> In the name of God, the Merciful, the Compassion- ate, And make mention of Mary in the Scripture, when she had withdrawn from her people to a chamber looking East, and had chosen seclusion from them. Then We sent unto her our Spirit and it assumed for her the likeness of a perfect man. He said, 'I am only a messenger of thy Lord, that I may bestow on thee a faultless son.'

The Muslim lives by the *Koran*. It has been regarded as a small book containing limited instruction, but from the first rituals of birth on through to the end of life the *Koran* holds guiding principles.

The church service of thanksgiving for the harvest is one of the most popular of the year and in schools too the opportunity is taken to remember our good fortune and to think of those in this country and overseas who do know what it is to be in want. Both in church and school, harvest produce is displayed in tasteful arrangements, while songs, hymns, prayers and stories are used to make up a harvest programme. Afterwards, the gifts are perhaps taken to hospitals, children's homes or old people's homes. Sometimes the produce is sold and proceeds given to such charities as Christian Aid. John Betjeman, in his poem *Diary of a Church Mouse*, comments cleverly on the popularity of the 'Harvest Festival' through the eyes of a mouse who rather resents the fact that all the year round he has to scratch about to find something in the church to eat, but at harvest time

> . . . other mice with pagan minds
> Come into church my food to share
> Who have no proper business there.

The harvest ceremonies are reflections of rituals as old as man can recall, centuries before Christ, for they owe their origins it seems to man's need to do homage to the spirit of life itself which he believed to live in the crop to be harvested, whether it is corn or anything else. Early man felt that by cutting the crop to some extent he killed the spirit and he was obliged to go through some sort of ritual to secure the renewal of its life for the following season. Many ceremonies involved making a model, or effigy or doll, from the last sheaf of the crop to represent the continuation of life. It is interesting to note that even today 'corn dollies' are very popular and the practice of this craft is expanding rather than diminishing in spite of canned foods and frozen foods which tend to dull the impact of harvest time.

The harvest doll was sometimes the last complete sheaf, dressed in a woman's dress and bedecked with coloured ribbons and variously called the harvest queen, the kern baby, the neck, the corn doll. In Northumberland the doll was attached to a long pole and carried home by the harvester, then set up in a barn where it stood as a centre-piece for the festivities that followed. In some parts of Scotland it was called the Old Wife or Cailleac, while in the neighbourhood of Belfast in Ireland it was called the 'Granny'.

In Pembrokeshire, in Wales, one of the reapers used to carry the doll home while the others tried to snatch it away and poured buckets of water over him. If he got home safely he kept it until the spring sowing. Then he would produce the doll and feed it to the plough horse, or else mix whatever grain was left in the new seed to be sown. This was to ensure the continuation of the corn spirit from one year to the next. The feat of killing the spirit is also exemplified in the practice in some parts of sharing the cutting of the last sheaf so that no one reaper could be held responsible for the final cutting.

It is recorded that as recently as 1947 at Great Bardfield Church, near Braintree in Essex, three devices made from wheat, oats and barley were displayed at harvest time. They were a cross on the pulpit, an anchor and a heart on the screen. They represented Faith, Hope and Charity. The vicar at the time reported that 'the people now expect to see them'. These devices were made by Mr Fred Mizen of Great Bardfield and it is interesting to note that in the little folk museum at Great Bardfield there is an example of Fred Mizen's work on display.

The harvest custom known as 'Crying the neck' was common in Devon and has been revived in St Keverne in recent times. The ritual·is associated with the ancient belief that the corn spirit lives in the last swaithe to be cut and that responsibility for making the last cut must be shared. At St Keverne, the reapers divide into three groups gathered round the last patch of standing corn. The first group call, 'We have it', the second group call three times, 'What have you?' The third group call 'The neck' three times also. This last sheaf is carried to the farmhouse, plaited into a 'corn baby' and kept over the fireplace until the following spring when it is put into the ploughed field, where the corn spirit begins to live again.

This is the St Keverne modern version of the ritual practised in former days when the reapers closed in on the last standing corn and the women gathered round with excitement. As the last stalks fell, the oldest of the reapers gathered them in his hands and began to twist them and weave them into the likeness of a man, the harvest manikin. This was bound with ribbon at the waist and neck, with head bristling and arms out-stretched. The other reapers formed a circle around and, as the leader lowered the doll to the ground, so they bent lower and lower imitating him. With hats off the whole group broke into a long, drawn-out musical cry – 'The Neck'. While this cry was drawn out, they all raised themselves up, lifted high their hats with the doll held high in their midst. This was performed three times, but now they cried, 'The Neck, we have 'un'. Then they all flung hats in the air and danced around shouting, laughing and kissing the girls. One young man snatched up 'The Neck' and ran towards a farm where a girl stood with a pail of water. She had to fling the water over him as he entered the farm. Then followed a party with eating, drinking and dancing.

A writer in 1826 declares that in one evening he heard six or seven 'Necks', although some must have been four miles off. Laurence Whistler in 1947 reflects that these reapers of Devon might be lamenting the death of Osiris, the Corn Spirit mortally wounded by their sickles, driven back into the last ears, and there finally murdered – lamenting his necessary death and imploring his forgiveness and renewal of life next season.

Mechanisation has undoubtedly taken some of the romance out of this season, but it was not so long ago that the last loaded waggons drawn in by a team of horses, with garlands, ribbons and flowers, rolled back to the farm to begin the Harvest Home, with good food, dancing, singing and, to sum up, merriment. As the last wagon rolled to a halt a young reaper would shout:

> We have ploughed, we have sowed,
> We have reaped, we have mowed,
> We have brought home every load,
> Hip Hip Hip – Harvest Home!

Then the cakes and beer came out and – on with the dance. For this evening, master and labourer sat down with no distinction and there would be visitors from other farms, since the labourers from each farm helped out the other at this time.

Much of this disappeared with the replacement of horse by tractor. Yet such is our feeling for traditions and our ability to overlay customs with modern beliefs that Harvest Home is now linked with Harvest Thanksgiving.

The Church had for hundreds of years taken an interest in the Harvest customs. A peal of bells from the tower would greet the harvest, wheat and other produce had been blessed in the church and even the corn dolly was allowed to grace the church door, although it soon transformed itself into a cross. The Reformation discouraged this, but in 1843 the vicar of Morwenstow issued a notice inviting parishioners to receive the Sacrament in the bread of the new corn, and the Church's Harvest Thanksgiving was born. Thanksgiving is now often an Evensong service, but the church is decorated suitably all day long with 'all God's gifts around us'.

The start of harvesting, a period of hard work culminating in the Harvest Home, was marked by a day called Lammas-tide. This name is a corruption of the Saxon word 'Llaf-maesse' or 'Loaf mass'.

Whatever its history, the Harvest Festival today is one of the best-attended services of the church; John Betjeman's mouse is puzzled at this and declares:

> But all the same it's strange to me
> How very full the church can be
> With people I don't see at all
> Except at Harvest Festival.

There is another story about mice at harvest time and it tells how a group of children on their way to school had to pass a cornfield and in due course saw it ripen ready for reaping. The day came when the harvester, a modern automatic machine, started to cut the corn, leaving it bound ready to be carted away. The children were very amused to see that the farmer had left an area of corn uncut, deliberately going round these few square yards and leaving it standing untidily amid the flattened areas around. The young people called out to him and made unkind comments about his eyesight. Nevertheless the farmer went on with his work for the next few days and every day the children were amused by the patch of corn left uncut. Then one day as they passed by they saw that it had been cut, left to the very last. One of the boys met him some days later and asked him why he had left that patch till last. The farmer explained that as he approached that piece of the field with his machine he spotted that a pair of field mice had made a nest there and had a family of six new-born mice. He could not drive straight over them knowing that they would all be killed, so he skirted round the nest and left that tuft of corn standing. Each day he looked to see if they were there until about three days later he watched the nest and saw the parent mice lifting the young in their mouths, one by one, and carrying them to a safe place in the hedge. They had realised the danger and were saving the family. When all were safe, the farmer knew that he could complete his work.

The children learnt something about kindness to wild creatures and also learnt not to make fun of other people's actions without knowing the reason for them.

(*Hindu Festivals*)

These two Hindu festivals are festivals of light held in the autumn with Diwali falling twenty days after Dussehra, and altogether this is considered to be a festival season of about a month long.

Dussehra is devoted to the victory of Lord Rama over the Demon King, Ravanna, the victory of good over evil, while Diwali celebrates the return of Lord Rama to the throne, in the capital Ayodhya, after fourteen years of exile in the forests. Since Dussehra is celebrated as a victory day, it is customary to use this festival for thanksgiving to a weapon like a sword, or a horse, or vehicles, or even vocational tools. Some sections of the Hindu community also worship the goddess Durga during the nine days preceding Dussehra day.

Diwali is a three-day festival when homes are gaily lit and are specially decorated and freshly painted. Traditionally, mustard oil is burnt in earthenware lamps and it is said to have the power of cleansing after the monsoon season. Coloured candles are also used. In Hindu festivals, coloured lightbulbs often now replace these, much as wax candles on the Christmas tree have been largely replaced by coloured electric lightbulbs. In many ways the celebrations resemble those of the Christian festival of Christmas. A great deal of visiting friends and relatives takes place, together with the exchange of gifts, which are often new clothes if the presents are between members of a family. Sweetmeats in the form of specially made cakes and savouries are given to visitors and taken as gifts to a host if one is going to a party or other family gathering. The mother of a family spends many hours before the festival making hundreds of these delicacies. Exchange of cards is a common social courtesy.

A feature of the two festivals is a cycle of plays called *Ram Lila*, based on the epic poem *Ramayana* written about Rama, the popular incarnation of the Hindu god Vishnu. There are so many adventures in this epic that the presentation of the plays covering all the stories can take up to a month. On the last day of Dussehra a huge effigy of the Demon King Ravenna, 9 metres tall, along with effigies of his chief helpers, is erected in an open arena. At sunset a mock battle is staged, a flaming arrow goes flying at the figures, and the whole erection goes up in flames amid the sound of crackers fixed inside the effigies. There are thousands of spectators, many of them village people who have walked for great distances, or come by bullock carts, rickshaws or bicycles. The actors and story-tellers hold the audience spellbound, often bringing tears to the eyes of the onlookers or rousing them to frenzied shouting. How they enjoy the final moment of Rama's triumph. He is the complete, splendid character whose glory is shared by Sita, his wife, a supreme model of all feminine virtues.

In one of the stories, Rama, because of intrigues and plots against him by wicked men, has to renounce his kingdom and go into exile. He told his wife, Sita, to stay in the palace since life in the forest would be harsh and dangerous. However, Sita insisted on going with him saying, 'Whatever calls you away, I want to be with you. With you is Heaven, without you is Hell.'

Rama and Sita went into exile with Rama's brother, Lakshmana, but the opposing King Ravenna decided to capture Sita. He drew off the attention of Rama by sending him in pursuit of a magic golden-looking gazelle and while Rama was so occupied, Ravanna captured Sita and took her across the sea to Lanka.

Rama, dismayed at the loss of his wife, declared that he would kill whoever had taken her and asked for help from a vulture called Jatayu. This vulture, assisted by a whole army of bears and monkeys, came to help Rama and show him the way to where Sita was held prisoner. Hanuman, one of the monkeys, crossed the water secretly and returned with the news that Sita was so far unharmed. Rama was certain that he could defeat Ravanna, if only he could get across the sea which lay between him and Lanka. He asked the ocean to help and the ocean said that he would allow Rama to build a great bridge. Rama found a craftsman smith named Nala who, with the animals as labourers, with trees and boulders built a huge bridge. Even a little squirrel came along to help by rolling himself in the dust and then shaking the dust off to fill in the spaces between the wood and the stones. The other animals laughed at the poor contribution made by the squirrel, but Rama thanked the squirrel seriously and to show his gratitude stroked him gently. All Indian squirrels from that day to this have three yellow bands across their backs indicating the traces of Rama's fingers as he stroked that helpful squirrel.

After five days the bridge was made and the army moved forward with a noise that drowned the roar of the ocean. A terrible battle followed but by brave deeds and miraculous happenings the battle was won for Rama. Finally Rama and Ravanna met in single combat. Ravanna, sensing defeat, called up great monsters to help him but one by one they were slain by Rama's arrows. Then Rama took a special magic arrow given to him by Agastya, a wise man and magician. This arrow had a life of its own and had been made from sunlight and fire. Its weight was equal to that of a mountain, yet magically Rama was able to fit it to his bow. Rama took aim and shot the magic arrow straight into Ravanna's chest. The arrow killed Ravanna and then, still covered with the enemy's blood, flew back of its own accord into Rama's quiver. So the enemy of Rama died.

At first Rama would not take Sita back, being unsure whether she had been true to him. Because of this, Sita longed to die. Her funeral fire was lit and as she approached it to die in its flames she prayed to one of the great gods, Agni. She said, 'Just as my heart never leaves Rama, so, great god Agni, never leave me.' Sita stepped into the flames, but a moment later was seen to rise up out of the fire, seated in the lap of Agni. This was proof that she had never ceased to love Rama, and he took her from the fire to be his true wife and Queen once more. Then Rama and Sita returned to their own kingdom.

With such stories, and there are many of them, the story-tellers could always be sure of a moving response from their audiences and one can imagine how effective these stories can be when played out on a stage.

YOM KIPPUR AND SUKKOS
(*Jewish Festivals*)

September/October

> *Ye shall offer one kid of the goats*
> *for a sin offering.*
> Numbers 29 xi

The three joyful festivals of the Jews are Pesach, Shovuos, and Sukkos. The significance of these has changed through the history of these people. The festivals originated in ancient times when the Jews were nomadic shepherds, but later became a settled farming community in Palestine. As the Jews achieved a superior culture they separated the festivals from the seasons of the year and gave them a new religious context. From local small community revelry, the festivals emerged as great national historic and religious observances, although many of the customs can be traced to agricultural origins. In former times the festivals involved pilgrimage to the Temple in Jerusalem, but with the Jews scattered all over the world, the festivals developed two aspects, one observed in the local synagogue and one observed by the family in the home. One can see similar developments in the festivals of other faiths.

Religious teachers impressed on the Jews that the New Year, Yom Kippur, should begin with due solemnity, fasting would be the order of the day, with the emphasis on confession and forgiveness. Only then, with sins forgiven, could the 'new man' indulge in the revelry of Sukkos. Yom Kippur then is the day on which Jews confess their sins and errors and pray for forgiveness. Without intermediaries they address themselves to God through prayers and confessions. Jews regret the destruction of the Temple, but through their religious ideals and with new ceremonies in homes and synagogues, they carry on without the Temple service. Even so the Yom Kippur ritual of the Temple is not forgotten and the ancient order of the ceremonial is recited and made dramatic by cantor and congregation.

In the days of the Temple, the High Priest stood at the gate on the day before Yom Kippur to receive the animal sacrifices that were brought by the people. The courtyard of the Temple would fill with people and at dawn the service began with the call, 'The light of morning has reached Hebron'. After a prayer, the High Priest moved down toward the people where two goats of equal size and value were tethered. Then the High Priest drew in turn two tablets from an urn, one marked 'For Yaweh' (God), the other 'For azazel' (The scapegoat). When the lot was cast, a red cord was tied to the horns of the scapegoat. Ceremonially the sins of the people were transferred to the scapegoat. The goat was hurried out of the Temple while the people shouted, 'Hurry and go'. The goat was hastened out to a cliff edge. At the top of the cliff, half of the red cord was tied to the cliff edge, the other remained on the goat's horns. The goat was then driven over the edge, life passed out of him as did the sins of the people. Parts of the Torah (the Law) were read before the ceremony ended. The drama of this ancient ritual catches the imagination.

Yom Kippur, the holiest day in the Jewish year, has been largely misunderstood. Some incorrectly call it a black feast. Actually, it is a white feast, with people dressed in white and the Ark covered with a white curtain. It is an occasion when people come together and renew their covenant with God. This is when they make their major approach to Him. Atonement, which the goat symbolised, is really at-one-ment – at one with

God, and at one with one's fellows. So Jews repent of their sins, of the places where they have failed in certain things and resolve to do better the next year. There is a family feeling about it – a feeling of oneness with Jews throughout the world and throughout all generations. So Yom Kippur seeks not only the purification of the individual, but also of the Jewish people as a whole.

Five days after Yom Kippur comes the most joyous of the Jewish festivals called Sukkos, 'The Feast of Tabernacles'. Originally it marked the end of the year's agricultural work and was celebrated by a pilgrimage to the Temple with an offering of thanksgiving.

How lovely are Thy tabernacles O Lord of Hosts

the pilgrim would say, and

I was glad when they said unto me
Let us go unto the House of the Lord.

Inevitably, such gatherings of people at the end of the year's work were attended by a great deal of fun-making, eating and drinking. Indeed some of the more serious-minded protested at the extent of the merry-making.

In the last days of the Temple, joyful ceremonies went on all day from the pouring of water and wine on the altar in the morning to the fire observance with torch dances in the evening. These dances would go on all through the night while the immense torches seemed to light up the city.

Sukkos eventually lost the attachment it had to the life of nature and the seasons of the year and, while retaining its joyful character, it became associated with thanksgiving for the Torah – the first five books of the Bible. In some respects the ceremonial is similar to the Christian Harvest Festival with its religious emphasis on thanksgiving. In some synagogues a small tabernacle or tent is built on a platform and processions are formed with people carrying the traditional plants of citron, palm, willow and myrtle.

Originally the booths or tabernacles were functional. They were wattle cabins in which the harvesters lived during the time of the 'ingathering' or harvest.

ALL HALLOWS EVE (HALLOWE'EN)   *October 31st*
ALL HALLOWS DAY, ALL SAINTS DAY
(HALLOWMASS)   *November 1st*
ALL SOULS DAY   *November 2nd*

Coming closely together, these festivals have a common theme. In former times the souls that were thought to have returned to earth on Hallowe'en were prayed for on the two following days, All Saints and All Souls. These two days were grouped together with Hallowe'en under the general name of Hallow Tide.

During this season the Church remembers all who have died, whether remarkable for their sanctity and good works, or whether quite unremarkable people remembered only by those near to them, together with all the dead who otherwise are completely forgotten.

Many of the customs practised on Hallowe'en find little or no authority in the Church, and at no other time of the year are pagan and Christian observances so confused. Historically, the feasts of All Saints and All Souls are pre-Reformation, but the reformers found so many unChristian ideas about the dead around at this season that the feast of All Souls was removed from the Church Calendar. It was restored in 1928, when it was felt that superstition was no longer a real danger.

Many of the practices common today at Hallowe'en embrace pagan origins. Hallowe'en had been the eve of the Celtic New Year, the autumn festival in honour of the sun god in thanksgiving for the harvest. The central part of the ceremony was lighting a bonfire to the sun. The festival celebrated Samhain, the lord of death, at the dying of the year, when Samhain called together the souls of the wicked who were condemned to inherit the bodies of animals. In parts of Ireland until recent date

113

the festival was called Oidche Shamhna, the vigil of Saman. The Romans grafted on to this festival their own celebration of Pomona, goddess of fruit, in which nuts and apples featured in the games and activities, just as they do to this day on Hallowe'en.

Of this season, Hallowe'en has retained many of the pagan elements; a night for spirit walking and the consideration of black magic, a time for dressing up, wearing masks and telling stories of ghosts and witches. The games played even today are of immense antiquity. Nuts are roasted in the fire and apples are 'bobbed for'. The apples float in water and each person has to try to pick one out with their teeth. Good fortune for a year is assured the successful players. A variation on this game is to 'fork' the apples out. Another game was played with a stick revolving on a string. One end of the stick held an apple, on the other end was a lighted candle. Children stood in a circle with hands behind their backs and tried to grab the apple with their teeth as it came round. Faces and hair were often splashed with grease. Lighting at such parties should be by candlelight, not the brilliant candles of Christmas, but shaded, darker candles, often in lanterns made from mangolds, casting weird shadows on the walls. These were called Jack O' Lanterns.

Individual ceremonies have grown up in all parts of the country, one of the most interesting being held at Hinton St George, in Somerset. This is called Punky Night, probably marking the true beginning of winter, and is intended to encourage the sun to fulfil its promise of life again next spring. Bonfires, chants and vigorous dancing are important parts of the ritual, but the most essential element is the carrying of Punkies. These are lanterns made from hollowed out mangel-wurzels.

They are carried from door to door while the people sing and dance, hoping for a reward of a coin or a candle. This slightly mercenary aspect is found in other parts of the country where the players offer 'trick or treat' as an alternative choice for their victim. Invariably the victim pays up rather than suffer the trick. However, of recent years the United Nations International Children's Fund has encouraged collectors on this night of the year to divert contributions to its cause. This is an opportunity for a stronger Christian element to be infused in this festival.

In America Hallowe'en is celebrated in a very similar fashion. The children's games and competitions are the same and special sweetmeats are prepared. The dominant colour scheme is orange and black, with marzipan sweets in these colours and gifts, if given, are wrapped in orange-and-black gift paper.

All Saints Day is a celebration in honour of saints, known and unknown, recognising that through the centuries many devout Christians quite worthy of sanctification have not been named and numbered in the Christian calendar. It is a day when Christians are expected to attend the service of Eucharist or Communion. So far as the Western Church is concerned, the festival seems to have become part of the calendar in the 9th century and it is of particular interest that at the time of the Reformation this holy day was retained.

On All Souls Day the Church remembers all those who have died. A legend connected with the foundation of this festival is given in Peter Domiceni's *Life of St Odil*, *Abbot of Cluny*. Cluny is a town in east-central France.

A pilgrim returning from the Holy Land took ship for France and encountered a terrible storm. The ship was wrecked and the pilgrim cast on a desolate island inhabited by a holy hermit. From the hermit the castaway learned that amid the rocks around the island was a deep chasm leading down to purgatory where the souls of the dead waited until they were free of their wrongdoing on earth before proceeding to heaven. The hermit declared that the tortured voices came up to him complaining that Christians did not pray hard enough for them, making their progress to Paradise more difficult. In particular they needed the prayers of the monks of Cluny Abbey. The pilgrim was rescued by a passing ship and he hurried to tell Odilo, Abbot of Cluny, about his adventure. The Abbot immediately set aside the day after All Saints Day to be a day when All Souls were to be commemorated. In due course the more ignorant folk took the festival to mean that for one night the souls of the dead could visit them, and often families sat up, putting out little cakes called 'soul' cakes, together with wine, to refresh the souls of the dead when they returned. Candles were lit and the home made clean and tidy. They were not surprised when the wine was not drunk for the folk believed that the ghost could take breath from the wine, leaving it apparently unchanged. In parts of France people used to go to the cemeteries on this night and kneel bareheaded by the gravestones.

Nowadays, in many churches, people put forward the names of those they wish to be remembered and these names are recited one by one during the prayers for the dead.

Please to remember, the fifth of November.
Gunpowder, treason and plot.

What good fortune it is that just as winter seems to be setting in, the evenings are darker and sometimes foggier, summer holidays seem to have receded into the past, and Christmas is a long way ahead, then along comes Guy Fawkes Day as an excuse for a bonfire and a good deal of fun with fireworks and food. In all parts of England sometime that evening an effigy of Guy Fawkes is set on top of the fire and burnt in remembrance of that November 5th between three and four hundred years ago when the original Guy was himself burned to death – or was he? In fact, who was he? And why is his memory so disgraceful that young boys and girls all down the ages have sung:

Guy, Guy, Guy,
Poke him in the eye,
Put him on the fire top
And there let him die.

It all began with the Gunpowder Plot and, on the occasion when the plot was first devised, Guy was not even there. Queen Elizabeth the First had died, after a reign of about forty-five years, without marrying and so without a direct descendant. Elizabeth's Aunt Margaret had married a King of Scotland and her great-grandson James, who was already King of Scotland, now became King of England also – King James the First of the Royal House of Stuart. His mother, Mary Queen of Scots, had brought him up as a Roman Catholic, but he knew that in England the authority of the Roman

117

Church had been rejected and the Protestant Church of England had been established. Queen Elizabeth's Parliament had imposed fines on Catholics who refused to go to Protestant churches. James had promised that if and when he became King of England he would not impose these fines on the Catholics, but no sooner was he established in London than he even increased the fines. Naturally the Catholics were angry and disappointed but most accepted the situation. However, a small group of Catholic gentlemen felt so strongly about it that they decided to kill James and, if possible, a great number of the members of Parliament as well. They had to work in secret for they knew that not everyone, even among the Catholics, would want such extreme measures to be taken.

The originator of the Gunpowder Plot was Robert Catesby, a Northampton gentleman who had already been to prison for not paying fines imposed on him for failing to attend a church of the establishment. His simple plan was to put enough gunpowder under the House of Lords to blow it up, at a time when the King, Lords and Commons were all met inside. Then the succession to the throne would go to a Catholic who would end the payment of these objectionable fines and uphold the right of an individual to attend the church of his or her choice.

Catesby outlined the plan to John Wright and Thomas Winter who were both at first startled, but then agreed to enter into the conspiracy. They decided to gain the help and technical advice of Guido or Guy Fawkes, an Englishman who was then in the Netherlands. Guy was a gentleman of good family, son of a York lawyer who had been registrar and advocate of the consistry court of the cathedral in that city.

Guy was an expert in the use of explosives and had acted as such in the recent wars. He was a man of great piety, good-humoured, mild, generous and a fervent member of his church, which was Roman Catholic. It was his enthusiasm for his faith that led him into the plot. He was certainly not the ruffian he is often depicted. That impression was circulated after his death by his Protestant enemies.

He arrived in England in April 1604 and met the three conspirators at Catesby's lodgings. At that meeting there was also Thomas Percy, a relative of the Earl of Northumberland. They all took a solemn oath 'by the blessed Trinity' to maintain secrecy. They took this oath on their knees with hands on a sacred volume.

Meanwhile Catesby had discovered that a house adjoining the building to be blown up could be rented and this was done, the house being rented in the name of Thomas Percy. The plan was to dig a way through the wall between the cellars and place the gunpowder under the House of Lords where Lords and Commons would be assembled with the King on the opening of Parliament. Guy Fawkes would light a train of gunpowder which would act as a fuse while he made his escape.

Guy Fawkes took the name of Johnson and pretended to be a servant of Thomas Percy. The plotters also rented a house at Lambeth on the other side of the River Thames where the explosives could be stored until the day for the action came. To guard it they needed another man so Robert Keyes was sworn in.

One of the dangers in a plot of this kind is to allow too many people to know the plan, since any one of them could perhaps accidentally let the secret out. This was the mistake the conspirators made. As time went on, more and more people were involved to help. It became a huge project.

It was not until December 1604 that work began in earnest. The plotters assembled in the house at Westminster and laid in good supplies of food, tools and other equipment. They soon made a hole in the wall of their cellar, but came up against a stone wall separating them from their objective. This stone wall was 2.7m thick. If they were to get through by February, when Parliament was due to meet, they needed more help, so John Wright's young brother Christopher and Tom Winter's older brother Robert were included. Later, Guy Fawkes, when questioned, said that all the gentlemen took part in the digging and they all had pistols ready to fight to the death if they were discovered. They had arranged that on the death of the King, his daughter Elizabeth, then only eight years old, should be rushed to London and proclaimed Queen. Her grandson George became the first of the Hanoverian sovereigns fifty-five years later as George I. They also had a store of arms in a house in Warwickshire which could be used to arm those Catholics who rallied to their cause. Christmas 1604 came and went and the plotters were still thinking of the February Parliament when it was announced that the opening of Parliament was to be delayed until October. This pleased the conspirators as it gave more time and they gradually enrolled more and more fellow Catholics into the plot. Some of these newcomers were concerned that Catholic Lords and Members would also die when the explosion occurred, and indeed some of these would be close friends and relatives.

One morning the conspirators heard a loud rushing noise in an adjoining cellar but they discovered that it was only the owner shifting his coal because he was going to sell it before moving away. This cellar was immediately below the House of Lords, so Thomas Percy bought it from the owner who was moving and thus avoided a great deal of tunnelling work through the stone wall.

Within a month, two tons of gunpowder was brought across the Thames and placed in the cellar under the House of Lords. Stones, old iron and lumber was thrown on top of the gunpowder, together with brushwood and rubbish of all kinds.

The opening of Parliament was once more delayed until November 5th. Many more Catholics were enlisted to provide money and create armed risings in various parts of the country, including Francis Tresham who provided £2,000 towards the expense of the enterprise.

It had been agreed that Guy Fawkes should be entrusted with the actual firing of the gunpowder. A slow-burning match would give him fifteen minutes to make his escape, and a boat would take him across the river to Lambeth. Then by horse and boat he would reach safety in Flanders. Sir Everard Digby was to assemble a number of supporters at Dunchurch in Warwickshire, pretending that he was holding a hunting party. Princess Elizabeth lived nearby and they planned to kidnap her to secure her accession to the throne.

The question about the safety of Catholic Lords still worried many of the conspirators, but Catesby emphasised that no warnings should be given and that some innocent people must suffer for the cause. Francis Tresham was particularly concerned about his brother-in-law Lord Mounteagle. Ten days before the opening of Parliament Lord Mounteagle gave an unexpected party. During the course of the gathering a footman who had been sent out on an errand was given a note by a stranger in the street, to be delivered to his master. The note was taken to Lord Mounteagle who decided to have it read aloud by a certain Thomas Wood who was present. It said, 'My Lord, out of love I bear to some of your friends, I have a care of your preservation. Therefore I would advise you as you .tender your life to devise some excuse to shift off your attendance at this Parliament, for God and man hath concurred to punish the wickedness of this time'. The letter also referred to a terrible blow that Parliament should receive 'yet they shall not see who hurts them'. No one knows who wrote the letter but it is now generally believed to have been at least instigated by Francis Tresham. The warning was communicated to the Earl of Salisbury, and Thomas Warde, who had read the letter, informed his friend Thomas Winter who then informed Catesby that the plot was discovered.

Surprisingly, the plotters did not give up the scheme, so confident were they that it would succeed. Tresham denied all knowledge of the letter and Guy Fawkes reported that nobody had disturbed the cellar or its contents. The plot was to go ahead. On November 4th, Guy Fawkes made his way to the cellar and during the afternoon he was visited by Lord Mounteagle and the Lord Chamberlain who seemed to be on a routine tour of inspection. They asked Guy who owned the rubbish collected there. The rubbish was, of course, covering the gunpowder. Guy said that it belonged to Thomas Percy and he had ordered the fuel and rubbish to be stored there. The visitors went away, apparently satisfied.

Just before midnight on the eve of November 5th, Sir Thomas Knevet, a Westminster magistrate, and a number of assistants went secretly and suddenly to the House. Guy was quickly arrested and the gunpowder uncovered. Guy Fawkes had on his person a watch, slow-burning matches, touchwood and a dark lantern. The lantern can still be seen in the Bodleian Library in Oxford.

Guy Fawkes would not disclose the names of his colleagues even when James ordered him to be tortured in the Tower of London. The other conspirators soon knew that the plot was discovered and fled from London. They armed themselves and held out in a last stand at Holbeach, the home of Stephen Lyttleton, but it took little time for the forces of the Sheriff of Worcestershire to overcome them. Then Fawkes, under torture, gave the names of his fellows and he and they were duly tried and executed, not burnt. They were sentenced to be hung, cut down alive, drawn on hurdles through the street and then the bodies quartered. Guy Fawkes was so weakened by his torture that he was dead when cut down from the scaffold.

Not only Catholics, but men everywhere, in Britain and abroad, were horrified when news of the plot was circulated. In joy at the deliverance of the King and his Parliament, bonfires were lit everywhere and celebrations included burning Guy Fawkes. So it has been ever since that time.

Since that day, whenever the Sovereign journeys from Buckingham Palace to the House of Lords for the opening of a new Parliament, there is an escort of guards. Today they make a fine spectacle, but they are a reminder that there was a time when their purpose was truly to protect from possible conspiracy. Also since the abortive plot of 1605, before the Sovereign enters the Palace of Westminster, the Royal Guard of Yeomen make a thorough search of the premises lest any modern Guy Fawkes happens to be lurking around with intent to harm.

A good guy is life-size and should really be processed round before finishing up on top of the fire. Many guys are made weeks before November 5th and carried round in barrows, old carts and old prams as a source of income. The boys and girls accompanying them beg for 'a penny for the guy'. Inflation has hit this business as badly as any other and the youngster hopes now for a five-penny piece at least. Possibly a well-made Guy would be worth it, but all too often nowadays the request is made and no Guy is to be seen.

The firework manufacturers have been all too inventive and some years ago the number of bonfire night accidents reached alarming figures. Happily there are restrictions now which make the fireworks safer, and there is a growing tendency for major firework displays to be set up professionally, with no risk of danger to onlookers. This is to be encouraged. Bonfire Night parties are common and nowhere else does a 'baked in the jacket' potato taste so good as in the smokey atmosphere of a bonfire.

THANKSGIVING DAY *Fourth Thursday in November*
(UNITED STATES OF AMERICA)

The story of the Pilgrim Fathers is the story of the first settlement in the New World in what was to become the United States of America. Until 1620 English colonists had crossed the Atlantic in search of adventure or gain. The Pilgrim Fathers were a band of settlers who sailed from Plymouth, England, with the intention of making a new home where they could practise their own faith without danger of persecution.

To cross the Atlantic in those days was a dangerous enterprise involving four or five months' hard sailing and with the journey completed, the settlement was itself open to the dangers of the native 'Indians', the hazards of extremes of climate, and the difficulties of transforming the wild country into good farm land. Many expeditions set out only to be destroyed by the natives and even after James I came to the British throne in 1603, there was news that a colony of fifteen hundred settlers had been wiped out.

In England, the newly-established Church was intolerant of Roman Catholics on the one hand and the extreme Puritans on the other. Early in the 17th century a group of separatists in England set up their own illegal, independent churches in Scrooby and Gainsborough (Lincolnshire) but were threatened with fines and imprisonment. Some of them, in 1608, fled to Holland to avoid persecution and set up churches in Amsterdam and later in Leyden. Even so they felt shut off and in order to make a new start in freedom, the groups in England and Holland determined to cross the Atlantic and found a colony in America. In July 1620 they sailed in *The Mayflower* from Delftshaven. A famous painting by Arthur Cope illustrates the scene as a group of the Pilgrims are pushed offshore in a small boat, taking them out to *The Mayflower*. They put in at Southampton on August 5th and left Plymouth on September 6th.

After a difficult and dangerous crossing, they landed in America late in December. These English colonists had no thought of disloyalty to their mother country. They thought of their newly-adopted country as New England, and named their first town settlement Plymouth. Today this state is called Massachusetts.

Before landing, each Pilgrim signed an agreement to combine into a civil body and frame just laws as should be 'most meet and convenient for the general good of the colony into which we promise all due submission and obedience'.

The total number of Pilgrims, men, women and children, was 102. They were determined people who were going to establish a sound community, built on hard work and unselfishness. This was the small seed from which the great tree known as the United States of America has grown.

The area where they landed was not the easiest to cultivate and their first winter was a severe one, eating deep into what supplies they had brought with them. However, they laid out a little township with log huts and when spring came they began to farm and sow their crops. *The Mayflower* was taken back to England by its crew and when it sailed in the spring of 1621 not one settler returned to England. Perhaps it was fortunate that the local native Indians were themselves weakened by their own internal fighting and by sickness. The settlers were hardly troubled by them. The settlers were certainly fortunate in having as their leaders Governor Bradford

and, for defence, Captain Myles Standish, both excep-
tionally gifted men.

When, in the autumn, their harvest was gathered in,
the Pilgrims saw that it was successful and celebrated
their success with Thanksgiving to God. This celebration
became and still is an annual festival. There was at one
time an objection to it on the grounds that it was a relic
of Puritan bigotry, but Americans regard it now as a
time for religious services of Thanksgiving and for
family reunions.

The rock on which the settlers first set foot, Plymouth
Rock, lies on the harbour shore near the site of the first
houses in Leyden Street, now sheltered by a granite
canopy. Above the rock rises Coles Hill where the
Pilgrims buried nearly half their number during that
first severe winter. They sowed grain over the graves to
conceal their misfortune from the Indians. In 1855 some
human bones were discovered and these now have a
place of honour above the granite rock canopy. Burial
Hill, formerly a defence work called Fort Hill, contains
many graves of the early settlers and their descendants,
the oldest stone being dated 1681. Tablets mark the site
of the old fort, which was also a place of worship and a
watch tower; there is an obelisk to Governor William
Bradford. Pilgrim Hall is a large stone building with
many relics of the Pilgrims. These include a portrait of
Edward Winslow, one of the original *Mayflower* pas-
sengers, books, manuscripts, Governor Bradford's Bible,
copies of Eliot's Bible, and Myles Standish's sword.

In 1889 a national monument was set up with a 13.7
metres high pedestal, figures 11 metres high representing
the Pilgrims and others representing Morality, Education,
Law and Freedom. Marble relief frescoes tell the story of
the first settlement.

Thanksgiving Day (United States of America)

Throughout America, Thanksgiving Day is a religious festival with attendance at church on the previous Sunday. It is also a day of family reunion. Where it is impossible for members of a family to be present, greetings cards are sent to show that they are not forgotten and to indicate that if it had been possible the family would have been together. Houses are decorated in warm autumn colours featuring the cornucopia of harvest and winter and acorn squash. Squash is a kind of gourd. These are all symbols of thanksgiving for the plentiful harvest. On the first Thanksgiving Day, Indian corn was a basic ingredient of the main meal, but now it is used in the scheme of decoration, in all autumn colours.

Food for the occasion is important and traditional. The main meal of the day consists of turkey, ham, cranberry jelly, mashed potato and candied sweet potato, or yams. 'Turkey and all the trimmings' as the hotel advertisements put it. The main course is followed by pumpkin pie, mince-pie and whipped cream. If the family is aware of strangers with nowhere to go on that day, they will generally offer hospitality so that the stranger feels 'at home' for Thanksgiving. Schoolchildren perform pageants and carry out full-scale projects on the history of the Pilgrim Fathers. It is also, like New Year's Day in Britain, a day for football matches (American style) and many old rivalries are revived annually on the field; West Point versus Annapolis; college versus college, and so on.

Primarily, however, the emphasis is on Thanksgiving for all blessings, just as the early colonists gave thanks for their first harvest.

ADVENT
ST NICHOLAS DAY

Three to four weeks before Christmas

December 6th

The advent of our God.
With eager prayers we greet.
Advent Hymn.

Advent means 'coming' or 'happening', and the season is considered by the Church as a time of preparation for the great happening of Christmas, the birth of Jesus Christ. This short season comes as something of a relief after the succession of 'Sundays after Trinity' in the Prayer Book. There is a stirring of excitement with the promise of Christmas. Indeed, the prayer called the Collect for the Sunday before Advent contains the words, 'Stir up, we beseech Thee' and includes phrases such as 'bringing forth the fruit' and 'being plenteously rewarded'. No wonder it was referred to as 'Stir up Sunday', encouraging housewives to think about making Christmas puddings and children to start their list of things they would like for Christmas.

Observance of Advent is not now so marked as it used to be. In the north of England at one time it was customary for women to carry two life-size figures around, one to represent Jesus and one to represent Mary. They were called the Advent images and when they were paraded outside a house, some money was expected in return for carol-singing. If the Advent images did not visit a house, this was reckoned to be very unlucky.

In parts of Europe farmers employed children to run through the fields with fire brands to set alight any bundles of straw still standing. This was a ceremony symbolising penitence, but it also had a practical motive in chasing out vermin from the fields before the new seed was planted.

In Italy towards the end of Advent bands of musicians playing instruments like bagpipes travelled to all the nearby shrines of Mary. Tradition said that the shepherds who went to the table at Bethlehem played on similar instruments.

Within the season of Advent, on December 6th, comes the feast of Saint Nicholas, the patron saint of Russia and the special protector of children, scholars, merchants and sailors. The legend of his secret gifts to three daughters of a poor citizen who would not have made marriages without such assistance was the origin of the old custom of giving gifts in secret on the eve of St Nicholas Day. This custom was subsequently transferred to Christmas, when the American corruption of the Dutch form, San Nicolaas, became Santa Claus. The early Dutch colonists brought this custom to America.

Little is known about the saint who probably lived in the early 4th century A.D. and was at one time the Bishop of Myra. Under the Roman Emperor Diocletian he suffered imprisonment and torture, but when Constantine became Emperor he was released. There are nearly 400 churches in England dedicated to St Nicholas and in art he is often depicted with three children standing in a tub at his side. This seems to refer to the legendary occasion when Nicholas restored three children to life who had been murdered and concealed in a great salting tub.

Until it was abolished in the time of Queen Elizabeth I, there was a custom in cathedrals and churches to appoint a Boy-Bishop on St Nicholas Day whose rule lasted until Holy Innocents Day on December 28th. The boy was chosen and dressed in bishop's robes and allowed to preach in church or cathedral. Other boys took over the offices of chaplains and clergy and the whole group processed around the town. You can imagine that the whole ceremony gave rise to a great deal of fun, which in time led to considerable irreverence and the custom was abolished by law. Even so, some remnants of the ceremony persisted and even in the 19th century there are evidences of children being allowed to play in church on December 6th.

Drama is often the feature of festive celebrations, and the following legend of Saint Nicholas might well offer a good opportunity for it.

Many years ago, Nicholas was a wealthy man living in a small village in northern Europe where winters could be very hard indeed. He was well-liked in the village and he felt very sorry for the poor and the needy, although he knew that they would not accept from him what they, in their own pride, would call charity.

It was early December and already the ground was thickly covered with snow. No wheeled traffic could get about and the only way to travel was by sleigh drawn by reindeer. For many in the village it was not a 'merry' Christmas to look forward to. Nicholas knew that in one cottage where an elderly couple lived, the husband was very ill and needed medicines and good food that were beyond their meagre resources, now getting less every day since the man could not get out to his regular work. Not far from them lived a large family, a man, his wife and four children. The children were already saying what they wanted for Christmas, but there was little likelihood that the father could afford such gifts. Where could he find the money for a doll, a train set, a model ship, and a large box of building bricks? Nicholas also knew of a lonely woman whom he saw every day cutting wood and carrying it in baskets to her cottage in order to keep a fire going. He thought that this work was really too much for her. Then he had an idea. If the villagers would not accept gifts from him, why not give them secretly?

One night, probably December 6th, when all was dark and quiet in the village, he put on his outdoor clothes, big high boots with his red trousers tucked in, his thick, warm red coat with the white fur lining, and his warm, red bonnet with a white tassle. Dressed like that, with his white beard covering his chin, he looked for all the world like – can you guess?

He drew out his sleigh from his shed and harnessed up his reindeer. On the sleigh he packed sacks of food, toys and wood. Quietly, with only the slightest noise of a sleigh bell, he drove through the village, stopping only to leave bulging sacks on doorsteps. Then, as secretly as he went out, he drove back to his home, hardly able to speak for excitement.

The next morning the elderly couple woke and the husband was not so well. His wife set about making breakfast, wishing she had more firewood, some eggs, some bread and some meat, but knowing they would have to make do with a small fire and some potato soup. She wondered what sort of day it was and went to her front door to look out. At first she wondered what that old sack was doing on her doorstep. Then she looked inside and there were all the things she had wished for, medicines, fruit, bread, meat, cheese and eggs. She called out to her husband and then took in all the things that had been left on her doorstep in the sack. I can tell you now that the man started to get better from that day.

Nearby the father of the four children sat at his frugal breakfast wondering how he could get the materials to make the toys his children wanted. He might make a doll's house from some pieces of wood that he had piled outside. He opened the door to go out and see, when he almost fell over a large sack on the doorstep. 'Come and see what I've found', he called to the family, who came rushing out. There was a doll's house, a train set, a model ship and a box of building bricks, as well as a lady's shawl and a very jaunty man's cap. 'Christmas has come early', they all agreed.

They were making such a noise that the woman who lived on her own nearby was compelled to get up, although she had intended to stay in bed longer in order to save wood which was so hard to collect. She went over to her front door feeling very cross, but as soon as the door was open she saw sacks full of cut firewood, enough to last her for a month at least.

There were many happy, puzzled people in that village and the strange thing was that this happened every year from then on. Just before Christmas, about December 6th, every year presents appeared by the sackful as if from nowhere.

I rather fancy that after a time some people began to guess where the presents came from, but they didn't tell. Some secrets are worth keeping, aren't they?

ST CECILIA'S DAY

> *But bright Cecilia rais'd the wonder high'r*
> *When to her Organ, vocal breath was given,*
> *An Angel heard, and straight appear'd*
> *Mistaking Earth for Heaven.*

> J. DRYDEN

Saint Cecilia is the patron saint of music. She was martyred for her Christian faith in A.D. 176, under the Roman Emperor Marcus Aurelius. She was a high-born Roman of a Christian family. During the persecution of Christians under Marcus Aurelius, she and her husband were put to death. Over the house in Rome in which she is said to have lived and which contained her body, a great church has been built, the Church of St Cecilia Tristevere. The present church dates from 1599 when Stefano Maderno claims to have seen the body of the saint and carved the sculpture of her lying on her side. The inscription says, 'Behold the body of the most holy virgin Cecilia, whom I myself saw lying uncorrupt in her tomb. I have in this marble expressed for thee the same saint in the very same posture and body'.

Her connection with music is difficult to trace, although there are vague legends about her attracting an angel to earth by her singing, and another legend which says she sang at her martyrdom.

The 13th-century *Golden Legend* tells her story in some detail and this is the source of Chaucer's *Second Nun's Tale* which is of this St Cecilia who was condemned to be roasted to death in a dry bath. She reclined there coolly, so we are told, and the Emperor was compelled to send his executioner to cut off her head. He seems to have bungled the job, for it took three days for her to die. Even so, the only possible connection with music comes in the couplet:

> And while the organs maden melodie
> To God alone in hearte thus sang she.

On that flimsy evidence many, including Dryden, attributed to her the invention of the organ and thereby 'added length to solemn sounds'.

By the middle ages, guilds of musicians had adopted her as their patron and innumerable painters produced works showing her playing the lute or the organ, or other instrument.

In England at the time of the Reformation she went out of favour, for the Puritans suspected music as being as dangerous as a 'cup of poison'. This opinion seems to have inhibited celebration of St Cecilia's Day until 1683 when the programme included a church service and an entertainment, including an ode.

In 1683 The Musicians Company was formed to keep St Cecilia's Day in a worthy manner, and each year thereafter the company met at St Brides Church in London. Later they transferred the ceremony to St Paul's Cathedral where in 1907 a stained glass window was presented in honour of the saint.

In the 17th and 18th centuries several provincial cities held such festivals, notably Wells, Oxford, Salisbury, Winchester and Devizes. Dublin and Edinburgh have also staged celebrations.

These festivals have inspired such works as Purcell's Ode to words by Nicholas Brady and Jeremiah Clarke's Ode to words by Dryden, which was reconstructed in the form of *Alexander's Feast*. During the first decades of the 20th century the contributions do not seem to have had outstanding merit, but in 1942 Benjamin Britten, whose own birthday by a happy coincidence was November 22nd, composed an *Ode to St Cecilia*.

In 1946, after a public luncheon at which the Lord Mayor spoke and the Poet Laureate recited a poem, there was a service at St Sepulchre's and a concert at the Albert Hall, which the Queen attended. Two orchestras took part and works by Purcell, Elgar, Vaughan Williams and Walton were performed. The programme included Purcell's Ode of 1692.

Andrew, the brother of Simon called Peter, was one of the twelve apostles who followed Jesus. His name, in Greek, means 'manly' and before joining the twelve he had been a follower of John the Baptist. By trade he was a fisherman, working his boat from Capernaum on the Sea of Galilee. After meeting Jesus he gave up fishing, along with his brother Peter, to become a disciple. After Jesus' death he travelled in Asia Minor and along the Black Sea as far as the River Volga. Hence he became the patron saint of Russia. He was taken prisoner for being a Christian and condemned to death by crucifixion. Legend has it that he acknowledged that he was not worthy to die as Jesus had died and so elected to be crucified on a cross of the form 'crux decussata', or diagonal. This has come to be known as St Andrew's cross. In the Scottish flag it is white (for Andrew's purity) on a blue background (for the sea which he loved). His remains or relics were taken from Patros where he was buried to Constantinople. Andrew was canonized by the Church, that is to say he became a Saint, and was eventually adopted by the Scots people as their patron. His remains are said now to be on the spot over which St Andrew's Cathedral was built and round which the town of St Andrew's grew up.

There are many legends about the manner in which the relics of St Andrew came to rest in Scotland and one of the most attractive is the one that recounts how a group of monks set out from Constantinople to reach Scotland with the good news of Jesus Christ and to convert the Scots to Christianity. This was probably in the 6th century. They asked for the relics of some holy man to take with them as a protection from all the dangers of the voyage. These would include robbers on the road, pirates at sea, wild beasts in the forest, the hazards of weather with possible storms, floods, danger of shipwreck and so on. When one considers it, they were asking for pretty heavy insurance. However, they were given the relics of St Andrew and they set off on the journey. After months of travel by land and sea, they arrived on the west coast of Scotland where they buried the relics and set up an altar within a small church on that spot. This settlement they called St Andrews and the people around, on being converted to Christianity, declared St Andrew to be their patron saint.

Since then, Scots people all over the world celebrate St Andrew's Day, much as they celebrate Burns' Night.

Inevitably at such times stories are retold that illustrate the bravery and independence of the Scots. Many of these tales date back to the period when Scotsmen were contesting the claims of Edward I and Edward II to be Kings of Scotland and were themselves following their leaders of Independence including such great characters as William Wallace, Robert Bruce and the Black Douglas.

At one time Robert Bruce, now claiming to be King of Scotland met with many reverses and when Castle Kildrummie was taken Bruce heard at the same time that his wife had been captured and his brother executed. Bruce made his way in despair to a miserable dwelling at Rochrin. He was considering giving up all his claims and wondering whether to take himself off to the Crusades. Looking upward to the roof of the hut in which he lay, he saw a spider suspended at the end of a long thread, trying to swing itself from one beam to the next and, idly, Bruce counted how many times he swung himself across and failed to link up with the other beam. Six

times he saw the creature try without success and he
remembered that he had just fought six battles and lost.
'Now', thought Bruce, 'since I am not sure what is best
to be done, I'll be guided by the spider. If he tries again
and succeeds, I will go out to battle once more, but if he
fails, I'll go to the Crusades in the Holy Land.' The
spider, at that moment, made a great effort and succeeded
in reaching the beam and fastening his thread. Bruce
resolved to try his own luck once more and, whereas
before he had gained no success, so after that he suffered
no setback. Since that incident, there are many Scots
bearing the name of Bruce who will on no account kill
a spider.

A distinguished follower of Bruce was Good Lord
James of Douglas who fought fiercely to recover the
castles of Scotland that had fallen into the hands of the
English. The castle at Linlithgow, or Lithgow as it is
sometimes pronounced, was such a castle. The castle had
the usual defences, including huge gates to the only
entrance and a portcullis, a sort of door formed of
crossbars of iron like a grate. This heavy defensive
equipment could be let down rapidly in case of attack
on the castle. The portcullis also had iron spikes at its
base which crushed all that it fell upon as the portcullis
was let fall.

Not far from the castle lived a farmer called Binnock
who supplied the castle garrison with hay. He had been
ordered to supply some cartloads and the night before
they were due to be delivered he sent a party of his
friends as near as possible to the gates but hidden from
the English garrison. They were to come to his assistance
as soon as they heard the signal which was a shout, 'Call
all, call all!' He loaded a great waggon with hay, but in
the waggon, hidden by the hay and lying flat on their

faces at the bottom of the cart, were eight soldiers fully armed. He chose one of his bravest men to drive, carrying a hatchet in his belt. Binnock himself walked alongside the waggon. In the morning he approached Linlithgow Castle where the guards, seeing only two men with a load of hay, lifted the portcullis and opened the gates. When the cart was directly under the portcullis, the driver took the hatchet and severed the horses' harness. The horses, freed from their load, started forward, leaving the cart of hay under the portcullis. Binnock gave the signal by shouting, 'Call all, call all!' and with his sword, until then hidden under his farm coat, slew the gatekeeper. The English soldiers tried to shut the gates but the cart hindered them and when the portcullis was lowered, the grating caught in the hay and could not drop to the ground. The men hiding in ambush joined the soldiers who were hidden in the cart and the castle was taken.

Another tale is told of the taking of Roxburgh Castle on a holiday, Shrove Tuesday, when most of the English garrison was merrymaking. The wife of one of the English officers was sitting on the battlements singing to her child on her lap. She saw black objects moving about in the darkness below and thought they were cattle. In fact they were the approaching soldiers of the dreaded Black Douglas who scaled the walls without being detected.

The woman sang:

> Hush ye, hush ye, little pet ye,
> Hush ye, hush ye, do not fret ye,
> The Black Douglas shall not get ye.

From the darkness at her shoulder a voice said, 'You cannot be sure of that', and the woman felt a heavy hand on her shoulder. She turned to see Black Douglas himself. The castle was taken and many English died that night. Black Douglas saw to it that no harm came to the woman.

Sir Walter Scott, who tells this tale in *Tales of a Grandfather*, comments, 'I dare say she sang no more songs about the Black Douglas'.

Yet another legend tells that a group of English soldiers were approaching a castle held by the Scots. It was a black, moonless night and, since the English were wearing black cloaks over their uniforms, it was unlikely that the sentinels would be aware of the attack until too late. As it happened, one of the advancing soldiers, moving on hands and knees, put his hand on a thistle and gave a cry of pain. This alerted the garrison and the castle was saved. Perhaps this incident explains why the thistle is one of Scotland's emblems.

The other, and sometimes preferred, emblem is the heather.

I come with many sins from a far land,
O God, this sanctuary is Thy Sacred Place.
Prayer on entering gates of Mecca

The day of Hijrat celebrates the emigration of the Prophet from Mecca to Medina. This was the most significant event in the history of Islam and marked the beginning of the spread of the faith.

In Mecca, where Muhammad was born and spent the first fifty-four years of his life, the Muslims had been relentlessly persecuted, their lives constantly in danger. They were not permitted to form a community or practise their religion openly. All these problems were solved when Muhammad and his followers migrated to Medina. The people accepted Islam and recognised the Prophet as their guide and leader. Hijrat Day is celebrated by exchanging greetings, family reunions, and relating stories about the Prophet.

Even so, Mecca became the central sacred city of Islam and one of the five 'pillars' of the faith was that, where practicable, a Muslim should, once at least, make a pilgrimage to Mecca.

Three or four years after the flight from Mecca to Medina, the Prophet wrote, 'The first house founded for the people was that at Mecca, a blessed house and a guidance to the worlds'. Long before the days of Muhammad, Mecca was a privileged holy place for Arab pagan religions, with a centre point in a great holy of holies called the Ka'ba or Cube. The origins of this great monument are unknown, but legend tells us that a great black stone which forms part of the eastern corner of the building was brought by Gabriel to Abraham and that the stone now bears the imprint of Abraham's foot. The stone was originally white but has turned black because of its contact with the impurity of the world. Gabriel later transmitted the *Koran* or Holy Book of Islam to Muhammad. There are other stories about the origins of the Ka'ba. For the Muslim it is not only the centre of the world, but the centre of the universe. Non-Muslims are forbidden to view or share in the Pilgrimage and are also forbidden to enter the city at all. People from the Western world may only enter if they are Muslims, although some have penetrated the holy place by going in disguise, dressed as native people.

A recent building programme costing £70 million has expanded the Great Mosque so that 300,000 can gather in its court, all with a clear view of the Ka'ba. The Ka'ba stands almost exactly in the centre, measuring 12 metres by 10 metres. It stands about 15 metres high with a parapet round the edge of the roof. The Ka'ba is seldom opened and is dimly lit with the Black Stone built into a corner. The stone has split into three large and several small pieces now bound together with a silver band. The stone built into the wall is kissed by the pilgrims as they process round the Ka'ba.

Over a million pilgrims go there every year, with the number of members coming from abroad constantly increasing. This throng represents all nations and classes, but when pilgrims enter Mecca they must all dress alike, in two sheets of unsewn white cloth. Rich or poor, man or woman, all are equal in this ceremonial. Women are not veiled on pilgrimage. The rites recall two great events for the Muslim: the story of Abraham and the Farewell Pilgrimage of Muhammad shortly before he died.

The Patriarch Abraham travelled along the desert caravan routes, just as modern pilgrims do on their way to Mecca. Significantly he moved away from the worship of many pagan gods towards the worship of the One True God. His story is told in *The Koran*. Abraham can be recognised as the spiritual father of the three great monotheistic (belief in One God) religions, Christianity, Judaism and Islam. He settled not far from Mecca, in Hebron, where his tomb is venerated by Muslim, Jew and Christian.

Abraham had two sons, Isaac, whose mother was Sarah, and Ishmael, whose mother was Hagar. Isaac, from whom the Jewish nation is descended, was the favoured son, while Hagar with her son Ishmael was turned out of the home at Hebron. Hagar made her way towards Beersheba but could find no water. At her wits' end, she left the boy to die, but a well miraculously appeared and the boy and his mother were saved. The boy, Ishmael, was the father of the Arab race who have adopted the Muslim religion and the well is that at Mecca where every pilgrim stops to drink. Hagar's despair in her frantic search for water is recalled by the pilgrims who run to and fro between the hillsides of Marwa and Safa.

The high point of the Pilgrimage is the Feast of Sacrifice which recalls Abraham's willingness to sacrifice even his favoured son if need be. Muslim families will share their own food with poorer neighbours on this occasion.

Only those of the Muslim faith can really appreciate all that is meant by the 'hajj' or pilgrimage, but the words of a 9th-century pilgrim after his third pilgrimage to Mecca are most revealing. He said, 'On my first pilgrimage I saw only the Temple; the second time I saw both the Temple and the Lord of the Temple; and the third time I saw the Lord alone'.

CHRISTMAS –
THE MASS OF CHRIST

This is one of the two most important festivals in the Christian year, the other being Easter. Christmas, the festival celebrating the birthday of Christ, always falls on December 25th, the date agreed sometime in the 3rd century A.D. There had been other dates used but, since it was not possible to determine the date precisely, the Christian Church decided to accept a date close to the time of the year when former religious and pagan festivals had occurred.

The first recorded stories about the life of Jesus Christ were probably written about the middle of the 1st century by a historian, Josephus, who lived from A.D. 37 to A.D. 100 (approximately). We do know that Jesus was born in Bethlehem, probably in winter time, during the reign of the Roman Emperor Augustus, formerly the Octavian we find in Shakespeare's *Julius Caesar* and *Antony and Cleopatra*. Herod, son of Antipater, was King of Judaea. Herod had been a very shrewd statesman in his younger days but now, with advancing years and failing health, devoted his time to avoiding difficult situations and pleasing his seniors. We can understand his dismay on learning that a 'King of the Jews' had been born, not related in any way to his own family.

The Bible story of the birth of Jesus Christ need not be told here, but it is a joyous story whether read in the Authorised Version with phrases like 'and there were shepherds abiding in the fields', or in modern translations which prefer versions such as, 'In the countryside close by there were shepherds who lived in the fields'.

The Christian Church took pre-Christian festivals and overlaid them with the Christian story and so helped converts to move away from former beliefs with less difficulty; accordingly, present-day customs reach back into pagan times. Undoubtedly, men and women have always needed and enjoyed a holiday in the middle of the winter when the weather is at its worst and the countryman's working day is at its shortest.

The Romans celebrated the Saturnalia with fire, food and light (followed by the New Year celebration of the Kalends) with a day, which we can now identify with December 25th, dedicated to the Birthday of the Unconquered Sun, *Dies Natalis Invicti Solis.* This festival included good food, wine, singing and charades, while homes were decorated with coloured lamps and evergreens. The Norsemen and the Druids also held celebrations on the shortest day of the year, again not far off December 25th when the Norsemen feasted and lit fires, while Druids celebrated the festival of Nolagh in similar fashion. Not surprisingly, then, our Christian Christmas still embodies reminders of former beliefs.

Christmas is a great season for singing, and Carol Services and festivals became more elaborate and of higher standard vocally and instrumentally each year. Some less 'professional' singing is heard from our doorsteps as the 'waits' make their rounds and it is heartening to observe that more, shall we say, organised groups now come to our doors to collect for recognised charities. Originally the word 'wait' meant 'the watch', the townsman who called that 'all was well' and acted as watchman in the streets while others slept. The waits sometimes enlivened matters by singing their calls and even occasionally playing a little flute-like instrument. Christmas was a good occasion for the 'wait' to stand under the windows and sing a Christmas song, until rewarded by a coin or two for services rendered through the year.

Most churches and schools present the scene of the birth of Jesus in the form of a 'crib', in which the characters of Mary, Joseph, the Babe, angels, shepherds and wise men are represented by three-dimensional figures. This custom was not unknown in Roman times when dolls and effigies were often displayed at festivals. The beautiful crib of St Francis of Assisi in the 13th century was probably the most striking, since real animals and people took part in presenting the Nativity Scene. From earliest times the Christian Church has encouraged the use of Drama in worship, and presenting scenes in an arena or theatre has always been a popular way of celebrating a festival. Christmas has its own presentations usually called Nativity Plays. Indeed the ceremonial of the Mass is in itself a moving dance-drama. Christmas presents a wonderful opportunity to use Drama in celebration and there is a wealth of material available for all age groups. It is not difficult to write original Nativity Plays, seeking inspiration from the Bible story, or to use the scripts of mystery plays performed at places like York, Coventry and Wakefield, or to find more modern interpretations in dance and mime.

The decorations we use at Christmas to brighten up our homes in the darkest days of winter often have pre-Christian origins. In any case, we have to fall back on evergreens like holly, mistletoe and ivy, symbols of life, when all other plants seem dead. Holly may well have been a holy tree, reminding us of new life in its evergreen leaves, as well as reflecting on the prickly leaves as a reminder of the thorns in the crown which this same Jesus was to wear some thirty years later. The red berries also serve to tell us of the blood he was to shed. A reminder of Good Friday even amid the joy of Christmas. Americans have introduced a custom of hanging a holly wreath on the front door at Christmas. Mistletoe has its origin as a decorative item in pre-Christian days. It appears that in Norse legend, Loki, the evil God, made an arrow of the poisonous wood of a mistletoe branch which he used to kill Balder, the Sun God. The other gods brought Balder back to life and the mistletoe tree promised never to harm again, but rather to become a symbol of love. Perhaps that is why we now use mistletoe as an excuse for kissing.

There is hardly need to explain why we use candles so extensively at Christmas. To the pagans they represented the heat and light of the sun, which in successive days after Christmas was to increase in strength, while Christians see the candle as a symbol of Jesus, the sun and light of the world. Candles are also symbols of the truth. Nowadays, as lighted candles on a Christmas tree can be a fire hazard, little electric lightbulbs are used to represent them.

Since more and more people live in towns, it is not so easy to go out and cut evergreens for decoration and so, to give colour and warmth to the house, it became fashionable to introduce coloured paper garlands, together with angels, stars, and ornaments made from a variety of materials. This is a development that has come about during the past 100 years or so. Christmas cards are relatively new arrivals on the Christmas scene, being introduced not much more than 100 years ago. It is interesting to see how they are used nowadays to take the place of Christmas garlands and other decorations. Strangely, New Year cards were popular before Christmas cards appeared, but seem now to have been superseded.

It is easy to understand why we give each other Christmas presents. The wise men travelled to Bethlehem bearing gifts and the Christian tradition originated there. One modern development of this tradition is for appeals and collections to be made on behalf of charities so that individuals may feel that, however small the offering is, it will be going to make Christmas a happier time for children in need, folk who are ill, elderly and lonely people, and also help to improve the desperate plight of people in many lands.

The spruce or fir tree has not always been recognised as the Christmas tree. There is a record that in 1605 at Christmas time in Strasbourg fir trees were taken into houses and decorated with coloured paper and gold foil and sweets, but this custom was not introduced into England until the 19th century when it was popularised by Queen Victoria's husband, Prince Albert. Queen Elizabeth still gives two trees each Christmas to the Dean of St Paul's to display in the church, but the large one given to London by the people of Oslo each year is better known.

Then we come to the subject of food and the many kinds of dishes prepared for the feast. England is perhaps foremost in the world for special Christmas fare. In fact, we eat much less at Christmas than our medieval an-cestors. They ate enormous meals with great dishes like boars' heads, taken with a good deal of drink. During Puritan times, this was discouraged and the people were very pleased when the Stuart monarchy was restored and once more the festival became a feast. Pigs were popular because they grew fat on acorns during the autumn, while the wealthier sections of the population ate peacock.

When sailors journeyed to America, they returned

with turkeys, unknown until that time and, in due course, turkey replaced stuffed peacock. Fruit puddings were made in the shape of a ball, with flaming brandy all over them, a reminder of the festival's earlier association with the worship of the sun, which Christmas replaced. It was customary to leave little gifts or coins in the pudding as surprises for the lucky finders. Mince pies represent the cradle in which Our Lord lay at Bethlehem. Some people make a wish as they eat a mince pie, while others contend that a mince pie should not be cut. In the days, not so long ago, when the housewife mixed all the original ingredients for puddings, everyone in the family 'had a stir' at it and made a wish which would come true, if the wishes were not divulged to anyone else.

Christmas is a great time for story-telling, sometimes with a happy ending, sometimes with some reference to the first Christmas and often with a mysterious element in keeping with the time of the year.

One story I have often told, though I cannot now remember where and when I first heard it, seems to me to hold all these elements. It concerns a young boy, John, about ten years old who, having been before the courts for some offence or other and whom a period of probation had not deterred, was committed to what in those days was called an approved school. Most of the boys were going home for Christmas, but John's parents, who kept a greengrocery shop in Southwark, near London Bridge, had asked the school not to send him home until after Christmas, since they would be busy in the shop until late on Christmas Eve and would still have a lot of clearing up to do.

On Christmas Eve most of the boys set off early, clutching suitcases and parcels of presents for parents and friends, some of the presents being made in classroom or craftroom at the school. The last had gone by 10 o'clock and John wandered through the empty playrooms and classrooms feeling very downhearted. He did so want to go home for Christmas. A holiday later on would not be the same. Then an idea came to him, naughty perhaps, but understandable. He had enough money in his locker to get him to London – why not go? When he knew he was not observed, he went to his locker, collected his pocket money, put on his outdoor clothes, slipped out of the school and made his way to the station.

When his train steamed into London a thick fog had descended over the city – what was then known as a 'pea-souper', reminding one of a scene in Dickens' *Christmas Carol*. John could not see more than a yard or two in front of him and was frightened by the shouts and sounds around him. However, he was sure he could find his way out of the station, a few turnings to St Paul's Cathedral, through the churchyard, over London Bridge and just down the second turning on the left.

He set off and after a while realised he was at the gate leading to St Paul's churchyard. Now it seemed darker, for there was not the occasional street lamp light. He found himself off the path stumbling over gravestones. Whichever way he turned, he could not find the foot-path. Now he was really afraid and sat on a tombstone, sobbing. His crying must have been heard, for he heard a call from out of the fog, 'What's the matter – can I help?' 'Over here', called John, 'I'm lost.' 'Stay where you are my boy. I'll come over to you', said the voice.

Out of the fog strode a confident figure. The man seemed to ignore the fog and the falling darkness. Without a single hesitation or stumble this stranger made his way among the gravestones to where John was sitting. 'There, hold my hand and we'll soon have you out of here. Where do you live?' John told him and the man, indicating that he knew where that address was, set off again quite firmly holding John by the hand and directing him past any obstacles that loomed up in the darkness. Through the churchyard, along the next street, up to the kerb of the main road. Pausing only to listen for a moment the man led John straight across the main road, across London Bridge, down a side street and soon the pair stood outside the little greengrocer's shop with its lighted window striving vainly to pierce the blackness.

As the stranger and John pushed the shop door open John's mother came forward. John's parents were so glad to see him. They had not been so busy as expected and were themselves wishing that John was coming home for Christmas. While John's father telephoned the school to set matters right, John's mother was hearing how John had been helped by the stranger. She offered him money which he refused, nor would he even take a gift of fruit. Calmly and confidently he wished them all a happy Christmas and then went out through the door and away down the street.

John had been greatly impressed by the stranger and told his parents how safe he had felt with his hand held by that man. 'But', asked John, 'why does he carry a white stick?' 'Ah', replied mother. 'That is because he doesn't see with his eyes – he sees with his heart.'

For Christians it is a time of rejoicing, prayer and praise with, for many, a focal point in the service at midnight. It is a high point in the worship when, with the Christmas communion made, the worshippers in the first moments of Christmas Day join in the words, 'Yea, Lord, we greet thee, born this happy morning'.

The days after Christmas: *December 26th, 27th and 28th*
ST STEPHEN, ST JOHN, HOLY INNOCENTS

> *Good King Wenceslas looked out,*
> *On the feast of Stepehn.*
>
> J. M. NEALE

The first day after Christmas is dedicated to Saint
Stephen, the first man to be martyred for believing in
Jesus Christ. His story is told in Chapters 6 and 7 of the
Acts of the Apostles. His defence before the council
against the charge of blasphemy was so passionate,
defiant and compelling, that the members of the council
would hear no more but cast him from the city and
ordered him to be stoned to death. Those chosen to
carry out this horrible sentence took off their coats in
order to do this thing and laid them at the feet of a
young man standing there looking on. He minded their
clothes for them. His name was Saul, later to be re-
christened Paul. Chapter 8 of Acts begins with the
words, 'And Saul was consenting unto his death'.

The popular Christmas carol associated with St
Stephen, which is quoted above, is sung to a delightful
tune which started life as a spring carol of the 16th
century called 'Spring has now unwrapped the flowers'.
J. M. Neale in the mid-19th century borrowed the
melody and put to it his words recounting the legend of
Wenceslas, the charitable king who sets out with his
page to take food, wine and fuel to 'yonder peasant by
St Agnes fountain'. The words do not match the quality
of the melody, but the carol seems destined to be very
popular at Christmas time for many ages yet.

December 26th is also known generally as Boxing
Day. The origin of this name for the day after Christmas

Day is difficult to determine. It was customary for apprentices to take round to each of his master's clients an earthenware box in which to collect 'tips' in recognition of the apprentices' services through the year, and representatives of firms delivered 'Christmas boxes' to each other soon after Christmas. The local parson would deliver bread, cheese and beer to the paupers of the parish on this day, probably wrapped up in a box. It was also common practice for the farmer's wife to set apart a large pie to be cut up and distributed to families of labourers employed on the farm.

The most probable explanation for 'Boxing Day' is that this was the day on which the church alms box or 'poor box' was opened and the contents distributed to the poor of the parish. Some support was given to this theory in 1976 when Parliament met the problem of appointing days for public holidays since Christmas Day fell on a Saturday. In debate, Sunday the 26th was referred to as Boxing Day, and Monday and Tuesday were to be public holidays and were referred to as the days after Boxing Day. One member of Parliament intervened by correcting these statements with a pronouncement that Sunday, December 26th, could not be Boxing Day since in time past the parish priest was too busy to open the poor box on a Sunday and therefore when Christmas Day fell on a Saturday, Boxing Day had to be left until Monday. The House accepted this statement and from then on referred to the sequence of days for 1976 as Saturday, Christmas Day; Sunday, the day after Christmas; and Monday as Boxing Day. This is a very interesting example of how ancient usage can intrude upon modern practice.

Boxing Day often sees the start of the pantomime season, although in the 20th century the shows presented in the professional theatres are often no more than musical reviews paying only lip service to the stories advertised in the title. Pantomime has a much deeper significance in the history of the theatre, having its origins in the Commedia dell'Arte, the Italian improvised theatre of the 16th to 18th centuries.

The principal effect of Commedia dell'Arte in England was seen in the pantomime or Harlequinade and in Punch and Judy shows. Even after the sophisticated adult pantomimes of the English theatre, based on popular fairy tales like Cinderella, Puss-in-Boots and Dick Whittington, some respect was paid to real pantomime by adding an impromptu Harlequinade after the main presentation. This little comedy with Harlequin, Columbine, Pantaloon the clown and so on, using numerous swing doors and trap-doors, was still a part of English pantomime well into the 1920s. Recently there has been renewed interest in pantomime and one or two companies present this kind of improvised presentation to young audiences with considerable audience participation.

Another form of theatrical presentation with an even older ancestry, often to be seen at Christmas time, is the presentation of the Mummers' Play, probably as popular today in some parts as it has ever been, although it would be rash to affirm that the sequence has never been broken. The words are rarely written down, and if they were would not be kept to. The players are ordinary country folk, getting together to rehearse and then, at Christmas and other seasons, to present an ancient story that evokes the England of the Crusades and perhaps stirring more distant and primitive memories of man as the Slain God of the Winter Solstice, yet not so dead as to be able to live again with the coming lengthening days. The principal characters are Father Christmas, Turkey Snipe, Quack Doctor, Robin Hood and so on. There are as many versions as there are companies that present the plays.

The second day after Christmas has been devoted by the church to St John the Evangelist, the 'disciple whom Jesus loved' and the writer of the fourth gospel.

The third day belongs to the Holy Innocents and recalls the fury of Herod when he learned that the three wise men had found the child they looked for and had not returned to Herod's court to report the find. Fearing that should the child, born in the city of David, be a threat to his own authority, Herod ordered his troops to go into Bethlehem and kill all the boy children of two years and under. Joseph and Mary, however, had been warned of this danger in a dream and had hurried away across the frontier into the safe refuge of Egypt and only when they felt that the danger had passed did they go back to their own home in Nazareth. The story evokes memories of the Jewish captivity in Egypt when, fearing that the Jewish population was growing too numerous, the Pharaoh ordered all Jewish boy children to be killed at birth. Moses, of course, through the courage and ingenuity of his sister Miriam, was saved.

BOOK LIST

Standard Dictionary of Folklore, Mythology and Legend,
   Funk and Wagnall, N.Y.
Encyclopaedia Brittanica, Enc. Britt.
Folklore, Myths and Legends of Britain, Readers Digest.
Old English Sports, P. H. Ditchfield, E.P.
Old English Customs, P. H. Ditchfield, E.P.
English Festivals, Laurence Whistler, Heinemann.
The Golden Bough, Sir James Frazer, Macmillan.
English Social History, G. M. Trevelyan, Longmans.
Life of Buddha, H. Saddhatissa, Unwin Paperback
The Muslim Mind, Dr Charis Waddy, Longmans.
Hinduism, K. M. Sen, Penguin.
Muhammadan Festivals, G. E. von Grunebaum, Curzon
   Press
British Calendar Customs, Wright and Lones.
Festivals of the Jewish Year, Theodor H. Gaster.
A Year of Festivals, Palmer and Lloyd, Warne.
Christmas and its Customs, Christina Hale, Richard Bell.
Easter and its Customs, Christina Hale, Richard Bell.
Customs and Traditions, Joan Sabin, Blackwell.
Festivals, Anthology compiled by Ruth Manning-
   Sanders, Heinemann.
Year Book of Customs, Christine Chandler, Mowbray.
The New Testament and its Background, I–III, James
   Edwards, Blandford.

FURTHER SOURCE MATERIAL

EPIPHANY

Poems	*Journey of the Magi*	T. S. Eliot
	The Gifts of the Magi	O. Henry
Bible	Matthew 2	

SEASON OF LENT

Poems	*For Pancake Day*	Traditional
	Ballad of the Bread Man	C. Causley
	The Donkey	G. K. Chesterton
	The Killing	Edwin Muir
	Good Friday	Christina Rosetti
Bible	Matthew 16, 17, 21, 26 and 27	
	Mark 11, 14 and 15	
	Luke 19 and 22	
	John 12 and 18	

EASTER

Plays	*Christ in the Concrete City*	P. W. Turner
	Caesar's Friend	Dickson and Morrah
	A Man Dies	Hooper and Marvin
	The Vigil	Ladislas Fodor
	The Ladder	Peter Howard
Poems	*Easter*	Edmund Spenser
	Easter Even	Christina Rosetti
Bible	Matthew 28	
	Mark 16	
	Luke 24	
	John 20	

WHIT SUNDAY
Bible   Acts of the Apostles 2

SHOVUOS
Bible   Book of Ruth

ALL SAINTS AND ALL SOULS DAYS
Plays   *Michael*   Miles Malleson
         Rose and Crown   J. B. Priestley
         The Rising of the Moon   Richardson and
                                           Berney

Poems   *All Souls Nights*   W. B. Yeats
         Witches Charm   Ben Jonson
         Hallowe'en   Leonard Clark
         Spells   James Reeves
         All Souls Night   Frances Cornford

CHRISTMAS
Books   *A Christmas Carol*   Charles Dickens
         *A Child's Christmas in
            Wales*   Dylan Thomas
Short   *Roaring Camp*   Bret Harte
Stories *Christmas at Dingley Dell* Charles Dickens
and   (*Pickwick Papers*)
extracts Christmas extracts   Thomas Hardy
            (*Under the Greenwood Tree*)
         Christmas Carol episode   Kenneth Grahame
            (*Wind in the Willows*)
         Winter and Summer   Laurie Lee
            (*Cider with Rosie*)

Poems	*The Christmas Tree*	C. Day Lewis
	Twelve Days of Christmas	Traditional
	A Christmas Carol	Christina Rosetti
	Christmas at Sea	R. L. Stevenson
	Christmas Day in the Workhouse	G. R. Sims
	A Visit from St Nicholas	Clement C. Moore
	Christmas	John Betjeman
	The Oxen	Thomas Hardy
	Keepin' up o' Christmas	William Barnes
Plays	*Frost at Midnight*	A. Obey
	Murder in the Cathedral (Christmas Sermon)	T. S. Eliot
	Business of Good Government	John Arden
	Kings in Judea (*Man Born to be King*)	Dorothy Sayers
	Santa Claus	Christopher Hassell
	Coventry Nativity Play	I. Lee Warner
Bible	Birth of Jesus in Matthew, Mark and Luke	

INDEX